Secrets of Shiva How to Get Divine Blessing of Mahadev The Most Powerful Rituals and Mantras

Acharya Someshwarnath Shastri

pencil

ISBN 978-93-5610-472-3

Published in India 2022 by Pencil

A brand of
One Point Six Technologies Pvt. Ltd.
123, Building J2, Shram Seva Premises,
Wadala Truck Terminal, Wadala (E)
Mumbai 400037, Maharashtra, INDIA
E connect@thepencilapp.com
W www.thepencilapp.com

Author biography

Acharya Someshwarnath Shastri is a great scholar of oriental knowledge. He has sacrificed his life for recovering the hidden and destroyed ancient hindu knowledge and culture. He has travelled far off countries to recover these ancient rituals, tantra, Yogic traditions, occult studies, astrology, dharmasastra and other traditional knowledge. He has written many books in different languages, one of his best known books is

মন্ত্র তন্ত্র বিজ্ঞান (আধ্যাত্মিক ও জাগতিক সুখ লাভের গুপ্ত বিদ্যা) (Mantra Tantra Science (The Secret of Spiritual and Worldly Happiness), wriiten in Bengali language.

CONTENTS

Mystery of Kailash Mountain, the abode of Lord Shiva

In Hinduism, since God resides on Mount Kailash, it is forbidden to go there. According to Tibetan folklore, a Buddhist monk named Milarepa once reached the top of Mount Kailash. When he returned, he warned everyone not to go to God's house. In Hinduism it is the abode of God Himself. Kailash is the most attractive of the entire Himalayas. Not much is known about this mysterious and inaccessible mountain. Kailash, located 22,000 feet above the Tibetan plateau, is a sacred place for Buddhists as well as the Hindu community. This pyramid-shaped hill has many ancient caves and caverns. Where Buddhist and Hindu monks can meet. These monks have been doing austerities behind the scenes for many years. Many people travel to Manas Sarobar every year. However, due to the inaccessible natural environment, only a small number of people can complete the journey. However, no one has been able to climb the summit of Mount Kailash yet. Going there after a certain point is forbidden. In Hinduism, since God resides on Mount Kailash, it is forbidden to go there. According to Tibetan folklore, a Buddhist monk named Milarepa once reached the top of Mount Kailash. When he returned, he warned everyone not to go to God's house. In addition to Manas Sarbor, there is another amazing heart monster palm at the foot of Mount Kailash. At 14,950 feet, Manas Sarovar is the heart of the world's highest freshwater. Another surprise is that no matter how strong the wind is, the water of Manas Sarovar is always calm but the water of Rakshasatal is always turbulent. Mount Kailash is said to be the center of the earth. Many people say that after returning from Mount Kailash, their hair and nails suddenly become quite big. It is said that once some Siberian mountaineers entered the forbidden area of Mount Kailash. Immediately their age increased by several decades and they died of old age a year later. In 1999, Ernest Muldashev, a Russian ophthalmologist, decided to visit the area to unravel the mystery of Mount Kailash. His mountaineering team consisted of geologists, physicists and historians. They met many Tibetan lamas. Spend many months in the vicinity of Holy Kailash. He then wrote a book, Where Do We Come From? After an investigation, Ernest Muldashef concludes that there is actually a man-made pyramid on Mount Kailash, and that the pyramid was built in ancient times. He claimed that a large pyramid was surrounded by many smaller pyramids and that miracles happened there. After returning from there, Ernest Muldashif writes, 'In the stillness of the night comes the sound of a strange whisper from inside the mountain. One night I and two of my colleagues heard a rock reading. And this sound was coming from the belly of Mount Kailash. We thought there was someone else inside the pyramid. " He further wrote, 'Tibetan texts state that Shambala is a spiritual country, located northwest of Mount Kailash. It is difficult for me to practice this from a scientific point of view. However, I can clearly say that the area of Mount Kailash is directly related to the life of the earth. When we make a planned design by combining the kingdom of the ascetics, the pyramids and the stone mirrors, we get annoyed when we see that! Because that design was designed to spatially store DNA molecules. " Nikolai Romnov, a scientist who has studied the Kailash Mountains and its surroundings, and his team met with religious leaders at a Tibetan temple. He said that a miraculous power flows around Mount Kailash. Kailash is the most attractive of the entire Himalayas. Not much is known about this mysterious and inaccessible mountain. Kailash, located 22,000 feet above the Tibetan plateau, is a sacred place for Buddhists as well as the Hindu community. This pyramid-shaped hill has many ancient caves and caverns. Where Buddhist and Hindu monks can meet. These monks have been doing austerities behind the scenes for many years. Many people travel to Manas Sarobar every year. However, due to the inaccessible natural environment, only a small number of people can complete the journey. However, no one has been able to climb the summit of Mount Kailash yet. Going there after a certain point is forbidden. In Hinduism, since God resides on Mount Kailash, it is forbidden to go there. According to Tibetan folklore, a Buddhist monk named Milarepa once reached the top of Mount Kailash. When he returned, he warned everyone not to go to God's house. In addition to Manas Sarbor, there is another amazing heart monster palm at the foot of Mount Kailash. At 14,950 feet, Manas Sarovar is the heart of the world's highest freshwater. Another surprise is that no matter how strong the wind is, the water of Manas Sarovar is always calm but the water of Rakshasatal is always turbulent. Mount Kailash is said to be the center of the earth. Many people say that after returning from Mount Kailash, their hair and nails suddenly become quite big. It is said that once some Siberian mountaineers entered the forbidden area of Mount Kailash. Immediately their age increased by several decades and they died due to old age one year later. Evidence of ancient beliefs has also been found in modern research. Russian geologists claim that Kailash is not just a mountain. Rather its position is like an axis or axis. Many people think that the people of the planet Vine have come and made Kailash hill one step further. And this is a pyramid! The most amazing thing is that no one has been able to conquer Mount Kailash yet. Mountaineers from different countries of the world have tried. But none of their attempts were successful. Kailash has remained elusive. But this hill is not inaccessible. Mountaineers have conquered much more inaccessible peaks than this. But for some mysterious reason, Kailash is invincible to them. The word kailas originates from the word crystal in Sanskrit. Because the ice-covered Kailash looks like a crystal. In Tibetan it is called Gango Rinpoche. In Tibet, the Buddhist guru Padmasambhava is called Rinpoche. Mount Kailash is named after him. Money is a precious gem made of ice. There is an ancient legend in Tibet that Guru Millerpai could only set foot on the top of Kailash. When he returned, he forbade them to conquer the mountain. Because the only person who can go to the top is the one who has no skin. Modern mountaineers also say Mount Kailasa is extremely unclimbable. The reason for that is unclear. At the foot of Mount Kailash are Manas Sarovar and Rakshasatal. These two lakes are the source of some of the longest rivers in Asia. At 14,7950 feet, Manas Sarovar is the highest freshwater lake in the world. Strange creation of nature! Manas-Rakshas has two lakes side by side. But there is sweet water in that mind. And the monster salt water. The water of Manas Sarovar is calm. But the water of the monster rhythm is turbulent. It is said in Ramayana that this lake was created by Ravana, an ardent devotee of Shiva. There is something about the climate of Mount Kailash that makes people look old. In general, the rate at which human nails and hair grow if you spend at least 12 hours in the Kailash hills, this growth rate doubles. Mount Kailash, the abode of the meditating Mahadev, stands as the bearer and carrier of thousands of such wonders. Mount Kailash, the abode of Mahadev. The name Kailas has been familiar to us since childhood. In that case the place is also quite popular for traveling. But no one has been able to travel there till today. Although it is possible to travel to Amarnath by climbing a long hill, even if you climb Mount Everest due to its high altitude, the journey to Kailash is not a matter of one's hand. Many tried but failed. Invincible Mount Kailash 1. Near the summit of Kailash, many faced a severe storm and could not get up. 2. Many have been forced to come down in a hurry thinking that their own death is imminent. 3. The pyramid looks like Mount Kailash, surrounded by four rivers like the Hindu Shatadru. Many also say that it is the biggest pyramid in the world. Steep as a pyramid, so maybe no one could get up. 4. By the time you reach Kailash, your age is increasing very quickly! A Tibetan saint who was initiated in an attempt to travel to Kailash. But he failed. With how much age is increasing in an instant. Not only this, with the help of fire you can do welding. 5. Many people say that Kailash changes place so Kailash journey is not possible. . Scientists say there is no magnetic field in Kailash. That's why some compasses don't work. . No one could go to Kailash as God and Evil Lake were surrounded. Har-Parvati lives in Mount Kailash Traditional beliefs of Hinduism Let's find out now from our site! Not only Hinduism Kailash and Manas Sarovar are considered sacred places in Buddhist, Jain and forest religions. Six mountain ranges surround the Kailash hill like the petals of a lotus flower This 22,000 feet high black rock hill has been considered as the pillar of the earth since ancient times Which holds the mass of the earth Evidence of ancient beliefs has been found in modern research Russian geologists claim that Kailash is not just a mountain Rather its position is like an axis or axis Many people think that the people of Vine have come one step further and made Kailash hill And this is a pyramid! Related image The most amazing thing is that no one has conquered Mount Kailash yet Mountaineers from all over the world have tried But none of them succeeded Kailash has remained elusive But this mountain is not inaccessible Mountaineers have conquered much more inaccessible peaks than this But for some mysterious reason, Kailash is invincible to them Image result for mount kailash Origin of the word Kailas from Crystal in Sanskrit Because the ice-covered Kailash looks like a crystal In Tibetan, its name is Gango Rinpoche In Tibet, the Buddhist guru Padmasambhava is called Rinpoche Mount Kailash is named after him Meaning precious gems made of ice There is an ancient legend in Tibet that Guru Millerpai could only set foot on the top of Kailash. When he returned, he forbade them to conquer the mountain Because only he who has no skin can go to the top Modern mountaineers also say Mount Kailasa is extremely unclimbable The reason why is unclear Image result for mount kailash At the foot of Mount Kailash are Manas Sarovar and Rakshasatal These two lakes are the source of some of the longest rivers in Asia At 14,7950 feet, Manas Sarovar is the highest freshwater lake in the world Strange creation of nature! Manas-Rakshas have two lakes side by side But there is sweet water in that mind And salt water in the monster The water of Manas Sarobar is calm But the water of the monster rhythm is turbulent It is said in Ramayana that Ravana, an ardent devotee of Shiva, created this lake with austerities Related image Let's look at some of the Kailas-mysteries • This mountain in western Tibet is not only sacred to Hindus, but also Jains, Buddhists, the ancient 'forest' religion of Tibet — all consider Kailash sacred. According to the Tibetan Tantric tradition, Kailash is the abode of their god Demchamangya. According to Hindus, Shiva lives here. According to Jain thought, the inhabitants of Kailasa were their first Tirthankars. According to these three religions, climbing Kailash is forbidden. • At one time Russian experts described Kailash as a giant pyramid. They also say that this mountain is man-made. They refer to Kailash as the place of worship of a secret cult. A closer look reveals the pyramid shape of Kailash. Related image The Akalis of Europe attach special importance to Kailash. According to them, the position of supernatural energy here. According to many, this place is again the center of all supernatural. According to the Puranas, the four sides of Mount Kailash are composed of crystal, ruby, gold and lapis lazuli. This information is not true. But, the illusion of all these stones or metals falling in the light at different times of the day must create Kailash The shape of the lakes in the Kailash region is mysterious. Manas Sarobar is a full round water body. The shape of the monster palm is crescent shaped. Or they express the power of the sun and the moon. Image result for mount kailash • All that is known is that the 11th-century Tibetan emperor Millerpai was the only one to ascend Kailasa. There is something about the climate of Mount Kailash that makes people look old. In general, the rate at which human nails and hair grow if you spend at least 12 hours in Kailash mountain, this growth rate doubles. Mount Kailash, the abode of the meditating Mahadev, stands as the bearer of thousands of wonders. A Russian doctor visited Lake Kailash Man a few years ago. He claimed after the voyage that there was actually an ancient pyramid on Mount Kailash, and that the pyramid was surrounded by small pyramids. Its source is associated with the Pyramids of Giza and the Teotihuacan of Mexico. Mount Kailash, situated at an altitude of 8,618 m above sea level in the Himalayas, is considered a sacred place by Hindus, Buddhists and Jains. According to Hindu mythology, Lord Shiva lived on this mountain. And there he is buried. According to Tibetan Buddhists, the symbol of absolute bliss is Buddha Demchok (Dharmapala), the presiding deity of Mount Kailash. And in Jainism Kailas is called Ashtapada. According to them, the first Tirthankara, Ishvahadeva, found peace here. Related Articles Photo of Today's Horoscope 7th January 2022, People of Special Horoscope will see the face of profit Today's horoscope 8th January 2022, the people of special zodiac will see the face of profit 8 hours ago Photo of The star Indian cricketers are the most out for zero runs, a surprising name in the list The star Indian cricketers are the most out for zero runs, a surprising name in the list 10 hours ago To this day no human has been able to climb this mountain. The one who tried to climb this mountain died. And there is a lot of talk about it. The Chinese government, seeing the religious confidence of Mount Kailash, has banned climbing there. It is also said that some climbers tried to climb the mountain in the 19th and 20th centuries, but they all disappeared. Ernst Muldashev, a Russian doctor, wrote in his memoirs that he was once told by Siberian mountaineers that some climbers had reached a certain point on Mount Kailash. And a year later he died of old age. According to the famous Russian painter Nikolai Rerikh, there is a mysterious kingdom called Shambala around Kailash. Only ascetics live there. Ernst Muldashev In 1999, Ernest Muldashev, a Russian ophthalmologist, decided to visit the area to unravel the mystery of Mount Kailash. His mountaineering team consisted of geologists, physicists and historians. They met many Tibetan lamas. Spend many months in the vicinity of Holy Kailash. He then wrote a book, Where Do We Come From? After an investigation, Ernest Muldashef concludes that there is actually a man-made pyramid on Mount Kailash, and that the pyramid was built in ancient times. He claimed that a large pyramid was surrounded by many smaller pyramids and that miracles happened there. After returning from there, Ernest Muldashif writes, 'In the stillness of the night comes the sound of a strange whisper from inside the mountain. One night I and two of my colleagues heard a rock reading. And this sound was coming from the belly of Mount Kailash. We thought there was someone else inside the pyramid. " He further wrote, 'Tibetan texts state that Shambala is a spiritual country, located northwest of Mount Kailash. It is difficult for me to practice this from a scientific point of view. However, I can clearly say that the area of Mount Kailash is directly related to the life of the earth. When we make a planned design by combining the kingdom of the ascetics, the pyramids and the stone mirrors, we get annoyed when we see that! Because that design was designed to spatially store DNA molecules. " Nikolai Romnov, a scientist who has studied the Kailash Mountains and its surroundings, and his team met with religious leaders at a Tibetan temple. He said that a miraculous power flows around Mount Kailash.

Mount Kailash is described by Hindu mythology as the abode of Goddess Mahadev. This mountain in western Tibet is considered sacred not only by Hindus but also by Jains, Buddhists, the ancient 'forest' religion of Tibet. At 22,000 feet, the mountain is also unique in its appearance. The position of Manas Sarovar adjacent to this mountain above it has given another glory to each other. - Six mountain ranges are surrounded by lotus petals like Mount Kilas. This mountain has been considered as the pillar of the earth since ancient times, which holds the mass of the earth. ---- Emerging from this mountain is the source of life for a large population of Asia. Indus, Shatadru, Brahmaputra, Karnali (tributaries of the Ganges) - all formed from the vicinity of this mountain. This mountain was formed by the collision of the first continents. A volcano erupted in Lhasa Bay in Tibet at that time. The skin of the sea was breaking in the subduction of Eurasia (Eurasia = the common land of Europe and Asia). They were eroded, and the rest was formed by Mount Kailash. ---- There is something about the climate of Mount Kailash that makes people look old. In general, the rate at which human nails and hair grow কাট if you spend at least 12 hours in Kailash mountain, this growth rate doubles. Mount Kailash, the abode of the meditating Mahadev, stands as the bearer of thousands of wonders. --- The Akalis of Europe attach special importance to Kailash. According to them, the position of supernatural energy here. According to many, this place is again the center of all supernatural. --- According to the Puranas, the four sides of Mount Kailash are composed of crystal, ruby, gold and lapis lazuli. This information is not true. But, the illusion of all these stones or metals falling in the light at different times of the day must create Kailash. --- The most amazing thing is that no one has been able to conquer Mount Kailash yet Mountaineers from all over the world have tried But none of them succeeded Kailash has remained elusive But this mountain is not inaccessible Mountaineers have conquered much more inaccessible peaks than this But for some mysterious reason, Kailash is invincible to them --- Ancient Tibetan legend has it that the 11th-century Tibetan legend Millerpai was the only one to ascend Kailasa. Because only he who has no skin can go to the top Modern mountaineers also say Mount Kailasa is extremely unclimbable The reason why is unclear --- According to the Tibetan Tantric tradition, Kailash is the abode of their god Demchamangya. According to Hindus, Shiva lives here. According to Jainism, the inhabitants of Kailasa were their first Tirthankars. According to these three religions, climbing Kailash is forbidden. ---- Origin of the word kailas from the word crystal in Sanskrit Because the ice-covered Kailash looks like a crystal In Tibetan, its name is Gango Rinpoche In Tibet, the Buddhist guru Padmasambhava is called Rinpoche Mount Kailash is named after him Meaning precious gems made of ice ---- At one time Russian experts described Kailash as a giant pyramid. They also say that this mountain is man-made. They refer to Kailash as the place of worship of a secret cult. A closer look reveals the pyramid shape of Kailash. --- At the foot of Mount Kailash are Manas Sarovar and Rakshasatal These two lakes are the source of some of the longest rivers in Asia At 14,7950 feet, Manas Sarovar is the highest freshwater lake in the world Strange creation of nature! Manas-Rakshas have two lakes side by side But there is sweet water in that mind And salt water in the monster The water of Manas Sarobar is calm But the water of the monster rhythm is turbulent ---- The location of Kailash is at the Yarlang-Sangpo Treaty, where the Eocene continents met and transformed the surrounding sedimentary rocks. The vertical joint of the rock merged with this conglomerate to form a swastika on ice and rock. Swastika, a symbol of holiness, is practiced in almost all religions. Swastika, used by the Nazis in the last century. ---- Buddhism was brought to Tibet by Padmasambhava and the first Jain Tirthankara, both of whom attained enlightenment here. The people of the regional Tibetan forest religion call it the nine-story Swastika mountain ---- No ice accumulates at the very top, because its body is so steep. The ice falls down, melts, and those sacred rivers originate. In this desert-like area it stands as a white mountain, as the first and main range of the Himalayas. No one has reached its peak yet, although millions of pilgrims have wandered around it for thousands of years, hoping to find happiness in knowledge and rebirth. Many have repeatedly bowed and prostrated themselves, walking along the 50-kilometer track that surrounds it. The Chinese government has turned down an offer to climb to the summit by Reinhold Mysner, a world-famous mountaineering star.

Ardhanarishvarastotram

ardhanaareeshvarastotram
chaampeyagauraardhashareerakaayai
karpooragauraardhashareerakaaya .
dhammillakaayai cha jat'aadharaaya namah' shivaayai cha namah' shivaaya .. 1..
kastoorikaakunkumacharchitaayai
chitaarajah'punjavicharchitaaya .
kri'tasmaraayai vikri'tasmaraaya namah' shivaayai cha namah' shivaaya .. 2..
jhanatkvanatkankananoopuraayai
paadaabjaraajatphaninoopuraaya .
hemaangadaayai bhujagaangadaaya namah' shivaayai cha namah' shivaaya .. 3..
vishaalaneelotpalalochanaayai vikaasipankeruhalochanaaya .
samekshanaayai vishamekshanaaya namah' shivaayai cha namah' shivaaya .. 4..
mandaaramaalaakalitaalakaayai
kapaalamaalaankitakandharaaya .
divyaambaraayai cha digambaraaya namah' shivaayai cha namah' shivaaya .. 5..
ambhodharashyaamalakuntalaayai
tad'itprabhaataamrajat'aadharaaya .
nireeshvaraayai nikhileshvaraaya namah' shivaayai cha namah' shivaaya .. 6..
prapanchasri'sht'yunmukhalaasyakaayai
samastasamhaarakataand'avaaya .
jagajjananyai jagadekapitre namah' shivaayai cha namah' shivaaya .. 7..
pradeeptaratnojjvalakund'alaayai
sphuranmahaapannagabhooshanaaya .
shivaanvitaayai cha shivaanvitaaya namah' shivaayai cha

namah' shivaaya .. 8..
etatpat'hedasht'akamisht'adam yo bhaktyaa sa maanyo bhuvi deerghajeevee .
praapnoti saubhaagyamanantakaalam bhooyaatsadaa tasya samastasiddhih' .. 9..
iti shreematparamahamsaparivraajakaachaaryasya shreegovindabhagavatpoojyapaadashishyasya shreemachchhankarabhagavatah' kri'tau ardhanaareeshvarastotram sampoornam ..

bhootaadhipastotram

bhootaadhipam bhaje bhootaadhipam - divyabhootaadhipam bhaje bhootaadhipam .. 1
devaarimardanam bhootaadhipam bhoo-taganasuvanditam bhootaadhipam .. 2
devendravanditam bhootaadhipam - bhakta-vri'ndabahustutam bhootaadhipam .. 3
kaarunya veekshanam bhootaadhipam - shree-gajamukhasodaram bhootaadhipam .. 4
shreekund'alaanchitam bhootaadhipam shree-manikant'habhaasuram bhootaadhipam .. 5
naal'eekalochanam bhootaadhipam shree-kaalaambudashyaal'am bhootaadhipam .. 6
naanaartha daayakam bhootaadhipam kali-doshadaavaanalam bhootaadhipam .. 7
deenaarti bhanjanam bhootaadhipam su-bhaktajanataarakam bhootaadhipam .. 8
paand'yeshasevakam bhootaadhipam paand'ya-vamshasurakshitam bhootaadhipam .. 9
kleshapaashakshatim bhootaadhipam klisht'a-janarakshakam bhootaadhipam .. 10
samsaarataarakam bhootaadhipam shatru-kuladhvamsakam bhootaadhipam .. 11
punyalokaashrayam bhootaadhipam punya-janapoojitam bhootaadhipam .. 12
aashritavatsalam bhootaadhipam vishva-vishri'tavigraham bhootaadhipam .. 13
kalyaanadaayakam bhootaadhipam su-keertana sakta chittam bhootaadhipam .. 14
kiraatavapusham bhootaadhipam mri'ga-yaavanasthitam bhootaadhipam .. 15
ajnyaananaashanam bhootaadhipam su-vijnyaanadaayakam bhootaadhipam .. 16

adbhutavigraham bhootaadhipam ani-maadisiddhidam bhootaadhipam .. 17
samastaikanaatham bhootaadhipam taapa-trayashaantidam bhootaadhipam .. 18
bhootaadhipa stotram samaaptam ..

shiva sahasranAma stotram

mahaabhaarataantargatam
tatah' sa prayato bhootvaa mama taata yudhisht'hira .
praanjalih' praaha viprarshirnaamasangrahamaaditah' .. 1..
upamanyuruvaacha
brahmaproktairri'shiproktairvedavedaangasambhavaih' .
sarvalokeshu vikhyaatam stutyam stoshyaami naamabhih' .. 2..
mahadbhirvihitaih' satyaih' siddhaih' sarvaarthasaadhakaih' .
ri'shinaa tand'inaa bhaktyaa kri'tairvedakri'taatmanaa .. 3..
yathoktaih' saadhubhih' khyaatairmunibhistattvadarshibhih' .
pravaram prathamam svargyam sarvabhootahitam shubham .. 4..

shruteh' sarvatra jagati brahmalokaavataaritaih' .
satyaistatparamam brahma brahmaproktam sanaatanam .
vakshye yadukulashresht'ha shri'nushvaavahito mama .. 5..
varayainam bhavam devam bhaktastvam parameshvaram .
tena te shraavayishyaami yattadbrahma sanaatanam .. 6..
na shakyam vistaraatkri'tsnam vaktum sarvasya kenachit .
yuktenaapi vibhooteenaamapi varshashatairapi .. 7..
yasyaadirmadhyamantam cha surairapi na gamyate .
kastasya shaknuyaadvaktum gunaankaartsnyena maadhava .. 8..
kintu devasya mahatah' sankshiptaarthapadaaksharam .
shaktitashcharitam vakshye prasaadaattasya dheematah' .. 9..
apraapya tu tato'nujnyaam na shakyah' stotumeeshvarah' .
yadaa tenaabhyanujnyaatah' stuto vai sa tadaa mayaa .. 10..
anaadinidhanasyaaham jagadyonermahaatmanah' .
naamnaam kanchitsamuddesham vakshyaamyavyaktayoninah' .. 11..
varadasya varenyasya vishvaroopasya dheematah' .
shri'nu naamnaam chayam kri'shna yaduktam padmayoninaa .. 12..
dasha naamasahasraani yaanyaaha prapitaamahah' .
taani nirmathya manasaa dadhno ghri'tamivoddhri'tam .. 13..
gireh' saaram yathaa hema pushpasaaram yathaa madhu .
ghri'taatsaaram yathaa mand'astathaitatsaaramuddhri'tam. 14..
sarvapaapaapahamidam chaturvedasamanvitam .
prayatnenaadhigantavyam dhaaryam cha prayataatmanaa .. 15..
maangalyam pausht'ikam chaiva rakshoghnam paavanam mahat .. 16..

idam bhaktaaya daatavyam shraddadhaanaastikaaya cha .
naashraddadhaanaroopaaya naastikaayaajitaatmane .. 17..
yashchaabhyasooyate devam kaaranaatmaanameeshvaram .
sa kri'shna narakam yaati sahapoorvaih' sahaatmajaih' .. 18..
idam dhyaanamidam yogamidam dhyeyamanuttamam .
idam japyamidam jnyaanam rahasyamidamuttam .. 19..
yam jnyaatvaa antakaale'pi gachchheta paramaam gatim .
pavitram mangalam medhyam kalyaanamidamuttamam .. 20..
idam brahmaa puraa kri'tvaa sarvalokapitaamahah' .
sarvastavaanaam raajatve divyaanaam samakalpayat .. 21..
tadaa prabhri'ti chaivaayameeshvarasya mahaatmanah' .
stavaraaja iti khyaato jagatyamarapoojitah' .. 22..
brahmalokaadayam svarge stavaraajo'vataaritah' .
yatastand'ih' puraa praapa tena tand'ikri'to'bhavat .. 23..
svargaachchaivaatra bhoorlokam tand'inaa hyavataaritah' .
sarvamangalamaangalyam sarvapaapapranaashanam .. 24..
nigadishye mahaabaaho stavaanaamuttamam stavam .
brahmanaamapi yadbrahma paraanaamapi yatparam .. 25..
tejasaamapi yattejastapasaamapi yattapah' .
shaanteenaamapi yaa shaantirdyuteenaamapi yaa dyutih' .. 26..
daantaanaamapi yo daanto dheemataamapi yaa cha dheeh' .
devaanaamapi yo devo ri'sheenaamapi yastvri'shih' .. 27..
yajnyaanaamapi yo yajnyah' shivaanaamapi yah' shivah' .
rudraanaamapi yo rudrah' prabhaa prabhavataamapi .. 28..
yoginaamapi yo yogee kaaranaanaam cha kaaranam .
yato lokaah' sambhavanti na bhavanti yatah' punah' .. 29..
sarvabhootaatmabhootasya harasyaamitatejasah' .
asht'ottarasahasram tu naamnaam sharvasya me shri'nu .
yachchhrutvaa manujavyaaghra sarvaankaamaanavaapsyasi .. 30..

(atha sahasranaamastotram .)
sthirah' sthaanuh' prabhurbheemah' pravaro varado varah' . var prabhurbhaanuh'
sarvaatmaa sarvavikhyaatah' sarvah' sarvakaro bhavah' .. 31..
jat'ee charmee shikhee khad'gee sarvaangah' sarvabhaavanah' . var shikhand'ee cha
harashcha harinaakshashcha sarvabhootaharah' prabhuh' .. 32..
pravri'ttishcha nivri'ttishcha niyatah' shaashvato dhruvah' .
shmashaanavaasee bhagavaankhacharo gocharo'rdanah' .. 33..
abhivaadyo mahaakarmaa tapasvee bhootabhaavanah' .
unmattaveshaprachchhannah' sarvalokaprajaapatih' .. 34..
mahaaroopo mahaakaayo vri'sharoopo mahaayashaah' .
mahaatmaa sarvabhootaatmaa vishvaroopo mahaahanuh' .. 35..
lokapaalo'ntarhitaatmaa prasaado hayagardabhih' .
pavitram cha mahaamshchaiva niyamo niyamaashritah' .. 36..
sarvakarmaa svayambhoota aadiraadikaro nidhih' .
sahasraaksho vishaalaakshah' somo nakshatrasaadhakah' .. 37..
chandrah' sooryah' shanih' keturgraho grahapatirvarah' .
atriratryaanamaskartaa mri'gabaanaarpano'naghah' .. 38..
mahaatapaa ghoratapaa adeeno deenasaadhakah' .
samvatsarakaro mantrah' pramaanam paramam tapah' .. 39..
yogee yojyo mahaabeejo mahaaretaa mahaabalah' .
suvarnaretaah' sarvajnyah' subeejo beejavaahanah' .. 40..
dashabaahustvanimisho neelakant'ha umaapatih' .
vishvaroopah' svayamshresht'ho balaveero balo ganah' ..

41.. var balaveero'balo
ganakartaa ganapatirdigvaasaah' kaama eva cha .
mantravitparamo mantrah' sarvabhaavakaro harah' .. 42..
kamand'aludharo dhanvee baanahastah' kapaalavaan .
ashanee shataghnee khad'gee pat't'ishee chaayudhee mahaan .. 43..
sruvahastah' suroopashcha tejastejaskaro nidhih' .
ushneeshee cha suvaktrashcha udagro vinatastathaa .. 44..
deerghashcha harikeshashcha suteerthah' kri'shna eva cha .
shri'gaalaroopah' siddhaartho mund'ah' sarvashubhankarah' .. 45..
ajashcha bahuroopashcha gandhadhaaree kapardyapi .
oordhvaretaa oordhvalinga oordhvashaayee nabhah'sthalah' .. 46..
trijat'ee cheeravaasaashcha rudrah' senaapatirvibhuh' .
ahashcharo naktancharastigmamanyuh' suvarchasah' .. 47..
gajahaa daityahaa kaalo lokadhaataa gunaakarah' .
simhashaardoolaroopashcha aardracharmaambaraavri'tah' .. 48..
kaalayogee mahaanaadah' sarvakaamashchatushpathah' .
nishaacharah' pretachaaree bhootachaaree maheshvarah' .. 49..
bahubhooto bahudharah' svarbhaanuramito gatih' .
nri'tyapriyo nityanarto nartakah' sarvalaalasah' .. 50..
ghoro mahaatapaah' paasho nityo giriruho nabhah' .
sahasrahasto vijayo vyavasaayo hyatandritah' .. 51..
adharshano dharshanaatmaa yajnyahaa kaamanaashakah' .
dakshayaagaapahaaree cha susaho madhyamastathaa .. 52..
tejopahaaree balahaa mudito'rtho'jito'varah' . var 'jito varah'
gambheeraghoshaa gambheero gambheerabalavaahanah' .. 53..

nyagrodharoopo nyagrodho vri'kshaparnasthitirvibhuh' . var vri'kshakarna
suteekshnadashanashchaiva mahaakaayo mahaananah' .. 54..
vishvakseno hariryajnyah' samyugaapeed'avaahanah' .
teekshnataapashcha haryashvah' sahaayah' karmakaalavit .. 55..
vishnuprasaadito yajnyah' samudro vad'avaamukhah' .
hutaashanasahaayashcha prashaantaatmaa hutaashanah' .. 56..
ugratejaa mahaatejaa janyo vijayakaalavit .
jyotishaamayanam siddhih' sarvavigraha eva cha .. 57..
shikhee mund'ee jat'ee jvaalee moortijo moordhago balee .
venavee panavee taalee khalee kaalakat'ankat'ah' .. 58..
nakshatravigrahamatirgunabuddhirlayo gamah' . var layo'gamah'
prajaapatirvishvabaahurvibhaagah' sarvagomukhah' .. 59.. var sarvago'mukhah'
vimochanah' susarano hiranyakavachodbhavah' .. var susharano
med'hrajo balachaaree cha maheechaaree srutastathaa .. 60..
sarvatooryaninaadee cha sarvaatodyaparigrahah' .
vyaalaroopo guhaavaasee guho maalee tarangavit .. 61..
tridashastrikaaladhri'kkarmasarvabandhavimochanah' .
bandhanastvasurendraanaam yudhi shatruvinaashanah' .. 62..
saankhyaprasaado durvaasaah' sarvasaadhunishevitah' .
praskandano vibhaagajnyo atulyo yajnyabhaagavit .. 63..
sarvavaasah' sarvachaaree durvaasaa vaasavo'marah' .
haimo hemakaro yajnyah' sarvadhaaree dharottamah' .. 64..
lohitaaksho mahaakshashcha vijayaaksho vishaaradah' .

sangraho nigrahah' kartaa sarpacheeranivaasanah' .. 65..
mukhyo'mukhyashcha dehashcha kaahalih' sarvakaamadah'
. var mukhyo mukhyashcha
sarvakaasaprasaadashcha subalo balaroopadhri't .. 66..
sarvakaamavarashchaiva sarvadah' sarvatomukhah' .
aakaashanirviroopashcha nipaatee hyavashah' khagah' .. 67..
raudraroopom'shuraadityo bahurashmih' suvarchasee .
vasuvego mahaavego manovego nishaacharah' .. 68..
sarvavaasee shriyaavaasee upadeshakaro'karah' .
muniraatmaniraalokah' sambhagnashcha sahasradah' .. 69..
pakshee cha paksharoopashcha atideepto vishaampatih' .
unmaado madanah' kaamo hyashvattho'rthakaro yashah' .. 70..
vaamadevashcha vaamashcha praagdakshinashcha vaamanah' .
siddhayogee maharshishcha siddhaarthah' siddhasaadhakah' .. 71..
bhikshushcha bhikshuroopashcha vipano mri'duravyayah' .
mahaaseno vishaakhashcha shasht'ibhaago gavaampatih' .. 72..
vajrahastashcha vishkambhee chamoostambhana eva cha .
vri'ttaavri'ttakarastaalo madhurmadhukalochanah' .. 73..
vaachaspatyo vaajasano nityamaashramapoojitah' .
brahmachaaree lokachaaree sarvachaaree vichaaravit .. 74..
eeshaana eeshvarah' kaalo nishaachaaree pinaakavaan .
nimittastho nimittam cha nandirnandikaro harih' .. 75..
nandeeshvarashcha nandee cha nandano nandivardhanah' .
bhagahaaree nihantaa cha kaalo brahmaa pitaamahah' .. 76..
chaturmukho mahaalingashchaarulingastathaiva cha .
lingaadhyakshah' suraadhyaksho yogaadhyaksho yugaavahah' .. 77..

beejaadhyaksho beejakartaa avyaatmaa'nugato balah' .
itihaasah' sakalpashcha gautamo'tha nishaakarah' .. 78..
dambho hyadambho vaidambho vashyo vashakarah' kalih' .
lokakartaa pashupatirmahaakartaa hyanaushadhah' .. 79..
aksharam paramam brahma balavachchhakra eva cha .
neetirhyaneetih' shuddhaatmaa shuddho maanyo gataagatah' .. 80..
bahuprasaadah' susvapno darpano'tha tvamitrajit .
vedakaaro mantrakaaro vidvaansamaramardanah' .. 81..
mahaameghanivaasee cha mahaaghoro vasheekarah' .
agnirjvaalo mahaajvaalo atidhoomro huto havih' .. 82..
vri'shanah' shankaro nityam varchasvee dhoomaketanah' .
var nityavarchasvee
neelastathaangalubdhashcha shobhano niravagrahah' .. 83..
svastidah' svastibhaavashcha bhaagee bhaagakaro laghuh' .
utsangashcha mahaangashcha mahaagarbhaparaayanah' .. 84..
kri'shnavarnah' suvarnashcha indriyam sarvadehinaam .
mahaapaado mahaahasto mahaakaayo mahaayashaah' .. 85..
mahaamoordhaa mahaamaatro mahaanetro nishaalayah' .
mahaantako mahaakarno mahosht'hashcha mahaahanuh' .. 86..
mahaanaaso mahaakamburmahaagreevah' shmashaanabhaak .
mahaavakshaa mahorasko hyantaraatmaa mri'gaalayah' .. 87..
lambano lambitosht'hashcha mahaamaayah' payonidhih' .
mahaadanto mahaadamsht'ro mahaajihvo mahaamukhah' .. 88..
mahaanakho mahaaromaa mahaakesho mahaajat'ah' .
prasannashcha prasaadashcha pratyayo girisaadhanah' .. 89..

snehano'snehanashchaiva ajitashcha mahaamunih' .
vri'kshaakaaro vri'kshaketuranalo vaayuvaahanah' .. 90..
gand'alee merudhaamaa cha devaadhipatireva cha .
atharvasheershah' saamaasya ri'ksahasraamitekshanah' .. 91..
yajuh'paadabhujo guhyah' prakaasho jangamastathaa .
amoghaarthah' prasaadashcha abhigamyah' sudarshanah' .. 92..
upakaarah' priyah' sarvah' kanakah' kaanchanachchhavih' .
naabhirnandikaro bhaavah' pushkarasthapatih' sthirah' .. 93..
dvaadashastraasanashchaadyo yajnyo yajnyasamaahitah' .
naktam kalishcha kaalashcha makarah' kaalapoojitah' .. 94..
sagano ganakaarashcha bhootavaahanasaarathih' .
bhasmashayo bhasmagoptaa bhasmabhootastarurganah' .. 95..
lokapaalastathaa loko mahaatmaa sarvapoojitah' . var lokapaalastathaa'loko
shuklastrishuklah' sampannah' shuchirbhootanishevitah' .. 96..
aashramasthah' kriyaavastho vishvakarmamatirvarah' .
vishaalashaakhastaamrosht'ho hyambujaalah' sunishchalah' .. 97..
kapilah' kapishah' shukla aayushchaivi paro'parah' .
gandharvo hyaditistaarkshyah' suvijnyeyah' sushaaradah' .. 98..
parashvadhaayudho deva anukaaree subaandhavah' .
tumbaveeno mahaakrodha oordhvaretaa jaleshayah' .. 99..
ugro vamshakaro vamsho vamshanaado hyaninditah' .
sarvaangaroopo maayaavee suhri'do hyanilo'nalah' .. 100..
bandhano bandhakartaa cha subandhanavimochanah' .

sa yajnyaarih' sa kaamaarirmahaadamsht'ro mahaayudhah' .. 101..
bahudhaaninditah' sharvah' shankarah' shankaro'dhanah' . var shankaro'naghah'
amaresho mahaadevo vishvadevah' suraarihaa .. 102..
ahirbudhnyo'nilaabhashcha chekitaano havistathaa .
ajaikapaachcha kaapaalee trishankurajitah' shivah' .. 103..
dhanvantarirdhoomaketuh' skando vaishravanastathaa .
dhaataa shakrashcha vishnushcha mitrastvasht'aa dhruvo dharah' .. 104..
prabhaavah' sarvago vaayuraryamaa savitaa ravih' . var sarvagovaayuraryamaa
ushangushcha vidhaataa cha maandhaataa bhootabhaavanah' .. 105..
vibhurvarnavibhaavee cha sarvakaamagunaavahah' .
padmanaabho mahaagarbhashchandravaktro'nilo'nalah' .. 106..
balavaamshchopashaantashcha puraanah' punyachanchuree .
kurukartaa kuruvaasee kurubhooto gunaushadhah' .. 107..
sarvaashayo darbhachaaree sarveshaam praaninaam patih' .
devadevah' sukhaasaktah' sadasatsarvaratnavit .. 108..
kailaasagirivaasee cha himavadgirisamshrayah' .
koolahaaree koolakartaa bahuvidyo bahupradah' .. 109..
vanijo vardhakee vri'ksho bakulashchandanashchhadah' .
saaragreevo mahaajatruralolashcha mahaushadhah' .. 110..
siddhaarthakaaree siddhaarthashchhandovyaakaranottarah' .
simhanaadah' simhadamsht'rah' simhagah' simhavaahanah' .. 111..
prabhaavaatmaa jagatkaalasthaalo lokahitastaruh' .

saarango navachakraangah' ketumaalee sabhaavanah' .. 112..
bhootaalayo bhootapatirahoraatramaninditah' .. 113..
vaahitaa sarvabhootaanaam nilayashcha vibhurbhavah' .
amoghah' samyato hyashvo bhojanah' praanadhaaranah' .. 114.. var praanadhaarakah'
dhri'timaanmatimaandakshah' satkri'tashcha yugaadhipah' .
gopaalirgopatirgraamo gocharmavasano harih'. 115..
hiranyabaahushcha tathaa guhaapaalah' praveshinaam .
prakri'sht'aarirmahaaharsho jitakaamo jitendriyah' .. 116..
gaandhaarashcha suvaasashcha tapah'sakto ratirnarah' .
mahaageeto mahaanri'tyo hyapsaroganasevitah' .. 117..
mahaaketurmahaadhaaturnaikasaanucharashchalah' .
aavedaneeya aadeshah' sarvagandhasukhaavahah' .. 118..
toranastaarano vaatah' paridhee patikhecharah' .
samyogo vardhano vri'ddho ativri'ddho gunaadhikah' .. 119..
nitya aatmasahaayashcha devaasurapatih' patih' .
yuktashcha yuktabaahushcha devo divi suparvanah' .. 120..
aashaad'hashcha sushaand'hashcha dhruvo'tha harino harah' .
vapuraavartamaanebhyo vasushresht'ho mahaapathah' .. 121..
shirohaaree vimarshashcha sarvalakshanalakshitah' .
akshashcha rathayogee cha sarvayogee mahaabalah' .. 122..
samaamnaayo'samaamnaayasteerthadevo mahaarathah' .
nirjeevo jeevano mantrah' shubhaaksho bahukarkashah' .. 123..
ratnaprabhooto ratnaango mahaarnavanipaanavit .
moolam vishaalo hyamri'to vyaktaavyaktastaponidhih' .. 124..
aarohano'dhirohashcha sheeladhaaree mahaayashaah' .

senaakalpo mahaakalpo yogo yugakaro harih' .. 125..
yugaroopo mahaaroopo mahaanaagahano vadhah' .
nyaayanirvapanah' paadah' pand'ito hyachalopamah' .. 126..
bahumaalo mahaamaalah' shashee harasulochanah' .
vistaaro lavanah' koopastriyugah' saphalodayah' .. 127..
trilochano vishannaango manividdho jat'aadharah' .
bindurvisargah' sumukhah' sharah' sarvaayudhah' sahah' .. 128..
nivedanah' sukhaajaatah' sugandhaaro mahaadhanuh' .
gandhapaalee cha bhagavaanutthaanah' sarvakarmanaam .. 129..
manthaano bahulo vaayuh' sakalah' sarvalochanah' .
talastaalah' karasthaalee oordhvasamhanano mahaan .. 130..
chhatram suchchhatro vikhyaato lokah' sarvaashrayah' kramah' .
mund'o viroopo vikri'to dand'ee kund'ee vikurvanah'. 131..
haryakshah' kakubho vajro shatajihvah' sahasrapaat .
sahasramoordhaa devendrah' sarvadevamayo guruh' .. 132..
sahasrabaahuh' sarvaangah' sharanyah' sarvalokakri't .
pavitram trikakunmantrah' kanisht'hah' kri'shnapingalah'. 133..
brahmadand'avinirmaataa shataghneepaashashaktimaan .
padmagarbho mahaagarbho brahmagarbho jalodbhavah' .. 134..
gabhastirbrahmakri'dbrahmee brahmavidbraahmano gatih' .
anantaroopo naikaatmaa tigmatejaah' svayambhuvah' .. 135..
oordhvagaatmaa pashupatirvaataramhaa manojavah' .
chandanee padmanaalaagrah' surabhyuttarano narah' .. 136..

karnikaaramahaasragvee neelamaulih' pinaakadhri't .
umaapatirumaakaanto jaahnaveedhri'gumaadhavah' .. 137..
varo varaaho varado varenyah' sumahaasvanah' .
mahaaprasaado damanah' shatruhaa shvetapingalah' .. 138..
peetaatmaa paramaatmaa cha prayataatmaa pradhaanadhri't .
sarvapaarshvamukhastryaksho dharmasaadhaarano varah' .. 139..
charaacharaatmaa sookshmaatmaa amri'to govri'sheshvarah' .
saadhyarshirvasuraadityo vivasvaansavitaa'mri'tah' 140..
vyaasah' sargah' susankshepo vistarah' paryayo narah' .
ri'tu samvatsaro maasah' pakshah' sankhyaasamaapanah' .. 141..
kalaa kaasht'haa lavaa maatraa muhoortaahah'kshapaah' kshanaah' .
vishvakshetram prajaabeejam lingamaadyastu nirgamah' .. 142..
sadasadvyaktamavyaktam pitaa maataa pitaamahah' .
svargadvaaram prajaadvaaram mokshadvaaram trivisht'apam .. 143..
nirvaanam hlaadanashchaiva brahmalokah' paraa gatih' .
devaasuravinirmaataa devaasuraparaayanah' .. 144..
devaasuragururdevo devaasuranamaskri'tah' .
devaasuramahaamaatro devaasuganaashrayah' .. 145..
devaasuraganaadhyaksho devaasuraganaagraneeh' .
devaatidevo devarshirdevaasuravarapradah' .. 146..
devaasureshvaro vishvo devaasuramaheshvarah' .
sarvadevamayo'chintyo devataatmaa''tmasambhavah' .. 147..
udbhittrivikramo vaidyo virajo neerajo'marah' ..
eed'yo hasteeshvaro vyaaghro devasimho nararshabhah' ..

148..
vibudho'gravarah' sookshmah' sarvadevastapomayah' .
suyuktah' shobhano vajree praasaanaam prabhavo'vyayah' .. 149..
guhah' kaanto nijah' sargah' pavitram sarvapaavanah' .
shri'ngee shri'ngapriyo babhroo raajaraajo niraamayah' .. 150..
abhiraamah' suragano viraamah' sarvasaadhanah' .
lalaat'aaksho vishvadevo harino brahmavarchasah' .. 151..
sthaavaraanaam patishchaiva niyamendriyavardhanah' .
siddhaarthah' siddhabhootaartho'chintyah' satyavratah' shuchih' .. 152..
vrataadhipah' param brahma bhaktaanaam paramaa gatih' .
vimukto muktatejaashcha shreemaanshreevardhano jagat .. 153..
(iti sahasranaamastotram .)
yathaa pradhaanam bhagavaaniti bhaktyaa stuto mayaa .
yanna brahmaadayo devaa vidustattvena narshayah' .
stotavyamarchyam vandyam cha kah' stoshyati jagatpatim .. 154..
bhaktim tvevam puraskri'tya mayaa yajnyapatirvibhuh' .
tato'bhyanujnyaam sampraapya stuto matimataam varah' .. 155..
shivamebhih' stuvandevam naamabhih' pusht'ivardhanaih' .
nityayuktah' shuchirbhaktah' praapnotyaatmaanamaatmanaa .. 156..
etaddhi paramam brahma param brahmaadhigachchhati .. 157..
ri'shayashchaiva devaashcha stuvantyetena tatparam .. 158..
stooyamaano mahaadevastushyate niyataatmabhih' .
bhaktaanukampee bhagavaanaatmasamsthaakaro vibhuh' .. 159..

tathaiva cha manushyeshu ye manushyaah' pradhaanatah' .
aastikaah' shraddhadhaanaashcha bahubhirjanmabhih' stavaih' .. 160..
bhaktyaa hyananyameeshaanam param devam sanaatanam .
karmanaa manasaa vaachaa bhaavenaamitatejasah' .. 161..
shayaanaa jaagramaanaashcha vrajannupavishamstathaa .
unmishannimishamshchaiva chintayantah' punah'panah' .. 162..
shri'nvantah' shraavayantashcha kathayantashcha te bhavam .
stuvantah' stooyamaanaashcha tushyanti cha ramanti cha .. 163..
janmakot'isahasreshu naanaasamsaarayonishu .
jantorvigatapaapasya bhave bhaktih' prajaayate .. 164..
utpannaa cha bhave bhaktirananyaa sarvabhaavatah' .
bhaavinah' kaarane chaasya sarvayuktasya sarvathaa .. 165..
etaddeveshu dushpraapam manushyeshu na labhyate .
nirvighnaa nishchalaa rudre bhaktiravyabhichaarinee .. 166..
tasyaiva cha prasaadena bhaktirutpadyate nree'naam .
yena yaanti paraam siddhim tadbhaagavatachetasah' .. 167..
var ye na
ye sarvabhaavaanugataah' prapadyante maheshvaram .
prapannavatsalo devah' samsaaraattaansamuddharet .. 168..
evamanye vikurvanti devaah' samsaaramochanam .
manushyaanaamri'te devam naanyaa shaktistapobalam .. 169..
iti tenendrakalpena bhagavaansadasatpatih' .
kri'ttivaasaah' stutah' kri'shna tand'inaa shubhabuddhinaa .. 170..
stavametam bhagavato brahmaa svayamadhaarayat .
geeyate cha sa buddhyeta brahmaa shankarasannidhau ..

171..
idam punyam pavitram cha sarvadaa paapanaashanam .
yogadam mokshadam chaiva svargadam toshadam tathaa .. 172..
evametatpat'hante ya ekabhaktyaa tu shankaram .
yaa gatih' saankhyayogaanaam vrajantyetaam gatim tadaa .. 173..
stavametam prayatnena sadaa rudrasya sannidhau .
abdamekam charedbhaktah' praapnuyaadeepsitam phalam .. 174..
etadrahasyam paramam brahmano hri'di samsthitam .
brahmaa provaacha shakraaya shakrah' provaacha mri'tyave .. 175..
mri'tyuh' provaacha rudrebhyo rudrebhyastand'imaagamat .
mahataa tapasaa praaptastand'inaa brahmasadmani .. 176..
tand'ih' provaacha shukraaya gautamaaya cha bhaargavah' .
vaivasvataaya manave gautamah' praaha maadhava .. 177..
naaraayanaaya saadhyaaya samaadhisht'haaya dheemate .
yamaaya praaha bhagavaansaadhyo naaraayano'chyutah' .. 178..
naachiketaaya bhagavaanaaha vaivasvato yamah' .
maarkand'eyaaya vaarshneya naachiketo'bhyabhaashata .. 179..
maarkand'eyaanmayaa praapto niyamena janaardana .
tavaapyahamamitraghna stavam dadyaam hyavishrutam .. 180..
svargyamaarogyamaayushyam dhanyam vedena sammitam .
naasya vighnam vikurvanti daanavaa yaksharaakshasaah' .. 181..
pishaachaa yaatudhaanaa vaa guhyakaa bhujagaa api .
yah' pat'heta shuchih' paartha brahmachaaree jitendriyah' .

abhagnayogo varsham tu so'shvamedhaphalam labhet .. 182..

iti shreemanmahaabhaarate anushaasanaparvani daanadharmaparvani

asht'achatvaarimsho'dhyaayah' .. 48 ..

shreemahaadevasahasranaamastotram samaaptam .

shreekri'shnaarpanamastu .

shreeshivaarpanamastu .

Shri Shivapanchachamara Stotram

suvarnapadmineetat'aantadivyaharmyavaasine
suparnavaahanapriyaaya sooryakot'itejase .

aparnayaa vihaarine phanaadharendradhaarine
sadaa namah' shivaaya te sadaashivaaya shambhave .. 1..

sutungabhangajahnujaasudhaamshukhand'amaulaye
patangapankajaasuhri'tkri'peet'ayonichakshushe .
bhujangaraajakund'alaaya punyakaalibandhave
sadaa namah' shivaaya te sadaashivaaya shambhave .. 2..

chaturmukhaananaaravindavedageetabhootaye
chaturbhujaanujaashareerashobhamaanamoortaye .
chaturgunadvirasht'akaprakaarachitrakelaye
sadaa namah' shivaaya te sadaashivaaya shambhave .. 3..

sharannishaakaraprakaashamandahaasamanjulaa-
dharapravaalabhaasamaanavaktramand'alashriye .
karasphuratkapaalamuktavishnuraktapaayine
sadaa namah' shivaaya te sadaashivaaya shambhave .. 4..

sahasrapund'areekapoojanaikashoonyadarshanaa-
sahasvanetrakalpitaarchanaachyutaaya bhaktitah' .
sahasrabhaanumand'alaprakaashachakradaayine
sadaa namah' shivaaya te sadaashivaaya shambhave .. 5..

sahasrahallaveerabhadrasimhanaadagarjitaa
shrutiprabhedadakshayaagabho??smanaa .
(??)
sadaa namah' shivaaya te sadaashivaaya shambhave .. 6..

rasaarathaaya ramyapatrabhri'drathaangapaanaye
dharaadharendrachaapashinjineekri'taanilaashine .
susaaratheekri'taanujaanu vedaroopavaadine
sadaa namah' shivaaya te sadaashivaaya shambhave ..

7..
mri'kand'usoonurakshanaavadhootadand'apaanaye
sukhand'amand'alasphuratprabhaajitaamri'taamshave .
akhand'abhogasampadarthalokabhaavitaatmane
sadaa namah' shivaaya te sadaashivaaya shambhave ..
8..
madhuripuvidhushakramukhyadevai-
rapi niyamaarchitapaadapankajaaya .
kanakagirisharaasanaaya tubhyam
rajatasabhaapataye namah' shivaaya .. 9..
.. iti shreeshivapanchachaamarastotram sampoornam ..

shiva stotra by Swami Vivekananda

om namah' shivaaya .
nikhilabhuvanajanmasthamabhangaprarohaah'
akalitamahimaanah' kalpitaa yatra tasmin .
suvimalagaganaabhe eeshasamsthe'pyaneeshe
mama bhavatu bhave'smin bhaasuro bhaavabandhah' ..
nihatanikhilamohe'dheeshataa yatra rood'haa
prakat'itaparapremnaa yo mahaadeva sanjnyah' .
ashithilaparirambhah' premaroopasya yasya
pranayati hri'di vishvam vyaajamaatram vibhutvam ..
vahati vipulavaatah' poorva samskaararoopah'
pramathati balavri'ndam ghoornitevormimaalaa .
prachalati khalu yugmam yushmadasmatprateetam
ativikalitaroopam naumi chittam shivastham ..
janakajanitabhaavo vri'ttayah' samskri'taashcha
agananabahuroopaa yatra eko yathaarthah' .
shamitavikri'tavaate yatra naantarbahishcha
tamahaha haramaud'e chittavri'tternirodham ..
galitatimiramaalah' shubhratejah'prakaashah'
dhavalakamalashobhah' jnyaanapunjaat't'ahaasah' .
yamijanahri'digamyah' nishkalam dhyaayamaanah'
pranatamavatu mam sah' maanaso raajahamsah' ..
duritadalanadaksham dakshajaadattadosham
kalitakalikalankam kamrakalhaarakaantam .
parahitakaranaaya praanavichchhedasootkam
natanayananiyuktam neelakant'ham namaamah' ..

Shivastotram Himalayakrita from brahmavaivarta puran

shreeganeshaaya namah' .
himaalaya uvaacha .
tvam brahmaa sri'sht'ikartaa cha tvam vishnuh' paripaalakah' .
tvam shivah' shivado'nantah' sarvasamhaarakaarakah' .. 1..
tvameeshvaro gunaateeto jyoteeroopah' sanaatanah' .
prakri'tih' prakri'teeshashcha praakri'tah' prakri'teh' parah' .. 2..
naanaaroopavidhaataa tvam bhaktaanaam dhyaanahetave .
yeshu roopeshu yatpreetistattadroopam bibharshi cha .. 3..
sooryastvam sri'sht'ijanaka aadhaarah' sarvatejasaam .
somastvam shasyapaataa cha satatam sheetarashminaa .. 4..
vaayustvam varunastvam cha tvamagnih' sarvadaahakah' .
indrastvam devaraajashcha kaalo mri'tyuryamastathaa .. 5..
mri'tyunjayo mri'tyumri'tyuh' kaalakaalo yamaantakah' .
vedastvam vedakartaa cha vedavedaangapaaragah' .. 6..
vidushaam janakastvam cha vidvaamshcha vidushaam guruh' .
mantrastvam hi japastvam hi tapastvam tatphalapradah' .. 7..
vaak tvam raagaadhidevee tvam tatkartaa tadguruh' svayam .
aho sarasvateebeejam kastvaam stotumiheshvarah' .. 8..
ityevamuktvaashailendrastasthau dhri'tvaa padaambujam .
tatrovaasa tamaabodhya chaavaruhya vri'shaachchhivah' .. 9..
stotrametanmahaapunyam trisandhyam yah' pat'hennarah' .
muchyate sarvapaapebhyo bhayebhyashcha bhavaarnave .. 10..
aputro labhate putram maasamekam pat'hedyadi .
bhaaryaaheeno labhedbhaaryaam susheelaam sumanoharaam .. 11..

chirakaalagatam vastu labhate sahasaa dhruvam .. 12..
raajyabhrasht'o labhedraajyam shankarasya prasaadatah' .
kaaraagaare shmashaane cha shatrugraste'tisankat'e .
gabheere'tijalaakeerne bhagnapote vishaadane .. 13..
ranamadhye mahaabheete himsrajantusamanvite .
sarvato muchyate stutvaa shankarasya prasaadatah' .. 14..
iti shreebrahmavaivarte mahaapuraane shreekri'shnajanmakhand'e
himaalayakri'tam shivastotram sampoornam ..

Shukra Stava

asya shreeshukrastavaraajasya prajaapatih' ri'shih' anusht'up chhandah'
shukro devataa shreeshukrapreetyarthe paat'he viniyogah' ..
namaste bhaargavashresht'ha daityadaanavapoojita .
vri'sht'irodhaprakartre cha vri'sht'ikartre namo namah' .. 1..

devayaanipatistubhyam vedavedaangapaaraga .
parena tapasaa shuddhah' shankaro lokasundarah' .. 2..
praaptau vidyaam jeevanaakhyaam tasmai shukraatmane namah' .
namastasmai bhagavate bhri'guputraaya vedhase .. 3..
taaraamand'alamadhyastha svabhaasaabhaasitaambarah' .
yasyodaye jagatsarvam mangalaarham bhavediha .. 4..
astam yaate hyarisht'am syaattasmai mangalaroopine .
tripuraavaasino daityaan shivabaanaprapeed'itaan .. 5..
vidyayaa'jeevayachchhukro namaste bhri'gunandana .
yayaatigurave tubhyam namaste kavinandana .. 6..
valiraajyaprado jeevastasmai jeevaatmane namah' .
bhaargavaaya namastubhyam poorvageervaanavandita .. 7..
jeevaputraaya yo vidyaam praadaattasmai namo namah' .
namah' shukraaya kaavyaaya bhri'guputraaya dheemahi .. 8..
namah' kaaranaroopaaya namaste kaaranaatmane .
stavaraajamimam punyam bhaargavasya mahaatmanah' .. 9..
yah' pat'hechchhri'nuyaadvaapi labhate vaanchhitam phalam .
putrakaamo labhetputraan shreekaamo labhate shriyam .. 10..
raajyakaamo labhedraajyam streekaamah' striyamuttamaam .
bhri'guvaare prayatnena pat'hitavyam samaahiteh' .. 11..
anyavaare tu horaayaam poojayedbhri'gunandanam .
rogaarto muchyate rogaadbhayaarto muchyate bhayaat .. 12..
yadyatpraarthayate jantustattatpraapnoti sarvadaa .
praatah'kaale prakartavyaa bhri'gupoojaa prayatnatah' .
sarvapaapavinirmuktah' praapnuyaachchhivasannidhim ..

13..
iti shreebrahmayaamale shukrastavaraajah' sampoornah' ..

shukrastotram 2

shreeganeshaaya namah' .
shukrah' kaavyah' shukraretaa shuklaambaradharah' sudheeh' .
himaabhah' kuntadhavalah' shubhraamshuh' shuklabhooshanah' .. 1..
neetijnyo neetikri'nneetimaargagaamee grahaadhipah' .
ushanaa vedavedaangapaaragah' kaviraatmavit .. 2..
bhaargavah' karunaah' sindhurjnyaanagamyah' sutapradah' .
shukrasyaitaani naamaani shukram smri'tvaa tu yah' pat'het .. 3..
aayurdhanam sukham putram lakshmeemvasatimuttamaam .
vidyaam chaiva svayam tasmai shukrastusht'odadaati cha .. 4..
iti shreeskandapuraane shukrastotram sampoornam .

shukrastotram
atha shukrastotrapraarambhah' .
shri'nvantu munayah' sarve shukrastotramidam shubham .
rahasyam sarvabhootaanaam shukrapreetikaram shubham .. 1..
yeshaam sankeertanaannityam sarvaan kaamaanavaapnuyaat .
taani shukrasya naamaani kathayaami shubhaani cha .. 2..
shukrah' shubhagrahah' shreemaan varshakri'dvarshavighnakri't .
tejonidhirjnyaanadaataa yogee yogavidaam varah' .. 3..

daityasanjeevano dheero daityanetoshanaa kavih' .
neetikartaa grahaadheesho vishvaatmaa lokapoojitah' .. 4..
shuklamaalyaambaradharah' shreechandanasamaprabhah' .
akshamaalaadharah' kaavyah' tapomoortirdhanapradah' .. 5..
chaturvimshatinaamaani asht'ottarashatam yathaa .
devasyaagre visheshena poojaam kri'tvaa vidhaanatah' .. 6..
ya idam pat'hati stotram bhaargavasya mahaatmanah' .
vishamastho'pi bhagavaan tusht'ah' syaannaatra samshayah' .. 7..
stotram bhri'goridamanantagunapradam yo
bhaktyaa pat'hechcha manujo niyatah' shuchih' san .
praapnoti nityamatulaam shriyameepsitaarthaan
raajyam samastadhanadhaanyayutaam samri'ddhim .. 8..
iti shukrastotram samaaptam .

Shri Arunachala Ashtakam

shreearunaachalaasht'akam

darshanaadabhrasadasi jananaatkamalaalaye . kaashyaam tu maranaanmuktih' smaranaadarunaachale .. 1.. karunaapooritaapaangam sharanaagatavatsalam . tarunendujat'aamaulim smaranaadarunaachalam .. 2.. samastajagadaadhaaram sachchidaanandavigraham . sahasrarathasopetam smaranaadarunaachalam .. 3.. kaanchanapratimaabhaasam vaanchhitaarthaphalapradam . maam cha raksha suraadhyaksham smaranaadarunaachalam .. 4.. baddhachandrajat'aajoot'amardhanaareekalebaram . vardhamaanadayaambhodhim smaranaadarunaachalam .. 5.. kaanchanapratimaabhaasam sooryakot'isamaprabham . baddhavyaaghrapureedhyaanam smaranaadarunaachalam .. 6.. shikshayaakhiladevaaribhakshitakshvelakandharam . rakshayaakhilabhaktaanaam smaranaadarunaachalam .. 7.. asht'abhootisamaayuktamisht'akaamaphalapradam . shisht'abhaktisamaayuktaan smaranaadarunaachalam .. 8.. vinaayakasuraadhyaksham vishnubrahmendrasevitam . vimalaarunapaadaabjam smaranaadarunaachalam .. 9.. mandaaramallikaajaatikundachampakapankajaih' . indraadipoojitaam deveem smaranaadarunaachalam .. 10.. sampatkaram paarvateesham sooryachandraagnilochanam . mandasmitamukhaambhojam smaranaadarunaachalam .. 11.. .. iti shreearunaachalaasht'akam sampoornam ..

kiraatamoortistotram

namah' shivaaya bhargaaya leelaashabararoopine . prapannaartaparitraanakarunaamasri'naatmane .. 1.. pinchhottamsam samaaneelashmashruvidyotitaananam . udagraaraktanayanam gaurakausheyavaasasam .. 2.. kailaasashikharottungam chhurikaachaapadhaarinam . kiraatamoortim dhyaayaami paramam kuladaivatam .. 3.. durjanairbahudhaa''kraantam bhayasambhraantamaanasam . tvadekasharanam deenam paripaalaya naatha, maam .. 4.. mahyam druhyanti ripavo baahyaashchaabhyantaraashcha ye . vidraavaya dayaasindho chaapajyaanisvanena taan .. 5.. koot'akarmaprasaktaanaam shatroonaam shaatanaaya bhoh' . chaalaya chhurikaam ghoraam shatakot'isamujjvalaam .. 6.. vipaddaavaanalajvaalaasantaptam rogapeed'itam . kartavyataavimood'ham maam traayasva girishaatmaja .. 7.. namah' kiraatavapushe namah' kshemankaraaya cha . namah' paapavighaataaya namaste dharmasetave .. 8.. namo maheshvaryadaaya namo bhaktapriyaaya te . namo veeryanidhaanaaya namo gaureesutaaya cha .. 9.. namo namaste vishvaatman vishvamangaladaayaka . namo namaste sarvesha sarvashaktisamanvita .. 10.. raagadveshaadidurjantusankule manmanovane . vidhatsva mri'gayaam nityam vishisht'ashabaraakri'te .. 11.. yadyat karomi bhagavan manovaakkaayakarmabhih' .

bhavatprasaadattatsarvai bhooyaattvachcharanaarchanam .. 12.. iti shreevaasudevan elayathena virachitam kiraatamoortistotram sampoornam .

Shri Aghora Stava

sakalabhuvananaatham sarvadam sarvavandyam sahamanu manunaatham poojayitvaa sashaktim . paramashivamaghoraastraakhyamantraadhiraajam parimitavishayaabhirvaagbhirabhyarchayaamah' .. 1.. yatpaashasamhri'tishu paashupatam mahaastram granthiprabhedanavidhau kshurikaastramaahuh' . vighnastutau cha shakaleekarane shivaastram vande tadastramahamaishamaghorasanjnyam .. 2.. yaste bibharti nijamoordhani mantrachakram yo vaa bibhartyavayaveshu tadaksharaani . so'yam nirasya nikhilagrahabhootarogaan (heyam) jitvaastranaayakaripoonativri'ddhimeti .. 3.. vajram shaktirdand'akhad'gaahipaashaan vaayorastram saa gadaa(shankham?) cha trishoolam . padmam chakram saadhayanti svakri'tyam labdhvaajnyaam te digbhri'taamaayudhaani .. 4.. na bhavati vishapeed'aa naaripeed'aa na chaadhih' na khalu nikhilarogaa naapi bhootagrahaartih' . na dhanaharanabheetirnaabhichaarasya teshaam sakri'dapi bhuvane tvaam ye'straraajam smaranti .. 5.. mantree japaakusumasannibhabheemamoortim tvaam ghoramoordhaparipingalakeshapanktim . damsht'raakaraalavadanam tat'idaabhajihvam vyaattaananam ravishashijvalanogranetram .. 6.. naagendrabhooshanakapaalakri'taankamaalaa-shobhaanvitam bhrukut'ibhangakaraalavaktram . dhoomraambaram mukharanoopuramasht'abaahum dhyaayan prasidhyati jhanatkvanakinkineekam .. 7.. tvaam dakshinaih' karatalairasishoolamoola- shaktim(kteeh') d'amad'd'amarukam chashakam dadhaanam (?) . khet'am trishoolanri'kapaalasurendrashastraa-nyaarabdhayaatramarimardanamaashrito'smi .. 8.. karnadvaye karayuge bhujayoshcha yugme paarshvadvaye padayuge kat'imand'ale cha . kukshau gale shirasi naatha chaturdashaaheen tattadvibhooshanakri'taatmatanoorbibharshi .. 9.. vaame shooladale sthitastava harih' shreeneelarudrah' punarmadhye dakshinato vidhih' suphalake gauree guhah' kumbhake . dand'aagre gananaayako dinakaro dand'e'sya moole smarah' tenaaghaahigalagrahonmadaripoonastresha nirnaashaya .. 10.. tvaam saattvikam dhavalaroopamupaasya moksham sampraapnuvanti manujaah' sukhasannivisht'am . aaraktavarnamada(tha) raajasamuddhataanga- maa(saada)yanti sakalaabhimataarthasiddhim .. 11.. shatrukshayaaya sakalaamayanaashanaaya sarvopasargahataye cha tavaatiraudram . kri'shnam kri'paanilayataamasameva shastam yaanodyatam yativaraah' kathayanti roopam .. 12.. yadvaa damaddamarukaasipishaachashoola- moolaani dakshinakarairavaraih' kapaalam . tvaam khet'akena varaghant'ikayaa cha shoola- madhyam dadhaanamahamasht'abhujam namaami .. 13.. aakarshane nikhilarogahatau ripoonaam stambhe vasheekaranamohanadeepaneshu . yuddhodyatam tava pura(vapu)stat'idamshubheemam smri'tvogradamsht'ramachirena phalam labhante .. 14.. kri'shnaprabham trinayanam tribhujam tripaadam bheemam mahaashaniravam vikat'aat't'ahaasam . tvaam soochimusht'ihananairahibhooshitaangam dhyaayanti dhaavanaparam ripumaaranaadau .. 15.. tvaam shad'bhujam trinayanam shashikaantaroopam padmaananam vidhri'tabhooshanamoordhakesham . vaame kapaaladhanushee dadhatam sakhet'am shoolam sharam cha paratah' pranato'smi saasim .. 16.. vyaadhaadari(vari)pramathane sati bhoomikampe daahe dishaam prachuravri'sht'ishu chand'avaate . paapakshaye sakalavri'ddhishu shaantikaadau bheetau cha deva tava roopamidam smaranti .. 17.. sajalaghanaghanaabham bheemadamsht'ram trinetram bhujagadharamaghoram raktavastraangaraagam . parashud'amarukhad'gaan khet'akam baanachaapau trishikhanarakapaale bibhratam bhaavayaami .. 18.. shoolam moolam pishaacham sharamasisri'niyukt'ankayugbhind'ipaalam vajram tatsthoolamadhyam d'amarukamaparairghant'ikaam chaapakhet'au . paasham chakram cha dand'am bhujagamanalakam dakshinairbaahudand'ai- rmadhye tvaam vidyudaabham vijayinamanisham ghoranaatham bhajaamah' .. 19.. ke'pyasht'akaadhikasahasrakaram vidustvaa- manye'pi chaasht'ashatahastamatarkyavesham . kechiddvipanchakaramasht'abhujam pare'pi kechichchaturbhujayutam katichiddvibaahum .. 20.. kechidvadanti dhri'tashod'ashabaahudand'a- manye punardvinavasankhyakaraaravindam . tvaam sarvatah' prasri'tapaanipadam tu shaivam tejah' sudussahataram vayamaamanaamah' .. 21.. tvaam baahumoolavalayeekri'tatakshakaahim tanmadhyavesht'itamahaadri'd'hapoorvapadmam . paadaabjasamsthakulikam karapadmashobham dand'e kat'eeghat'itavaasukimekhalaankam .. 22.. tvaam shankhapaalabhujagendrakri'topaveetam jaanudvayasphuradanantamahoragendram . lootaadivri'shchikaviraajiviraajitaangam karkot'akaahiparibhooshitakant'habhaagam .. 23.. tvaam prasphurachchhikhinibhordhvakacham sphurantam ghoraananam vikri'taghorataraahibhoosham . vandaamahe varatanum vararoopashobham vakshollasachchat'achat'aaravarund'amaalam .. 24.. aamred'itaprayutasankhyatat'itkri'taasthi- maalaadharam kahakahaaravabhogibhoosham . bhooyo vamajjvalanadeeptalalaat'anetram tvaam hunkri'tena mama ghaataya ghaatayaareen .. 25.. chakroddhri'tapranavaphat'kri'tasamput'am te mantrottamam japati yah' samamangamantraih' . asmaatparam manushataih' kimihaalpasaarai-raayaatamisht'amanisham tvayi siddhimeti .. 26.. yah' panchashad'bhirdvidashaasht'ayugmairvarnairmanojnyaih' parikalpitaangah' . ri'shyaadikam beejasashaktikeelayuktyaatisanchintya japetsa dhanyah' .. 27.. yo mastake'likatale nayanadvaye cha madhye bhruvostava manoriha naasikaayaam . karnadvaye hanuyuge dvijapanktiyugme kant'he'sayoshcha jat'hare stanayoh' kramena .. 28.. varnaanniveshayati vakshasi naabhideshe baahuprakosht'hatalapaanishu vaamatashcha . sphijyoorujaanutalatashcharaneshu tadva- tpaayau salingavri'shane charamaangadeshe .. 29.. paarshvadvaye hri'di cha taaluni saadhakendrah' poojaavidhau japavidhau cha susampradaayah' . (so'yam nirasya) nikhilaartimanekasaukhyaa- nyaasaadayatyanimishairapi poojyamaanah' .. 30.. tvaam sheshakalri'ptavalayaankitapaanipadmam karkot'akaahiparibhooshitadaamashobham . vakshah'sthalaabharanatakshakanaagashobham padmaakhyanaagaparikalpitahaarabhoosham .. 31.. sushvetapadmapariklri'ptalalaat'ashobham madhyaangalagnakulikodarabandhanaagam . kechitkat'eeghat'itabhooshitashankhapaalam karnaavatamsavaravaasukimaamananti .. 32.. charmaasichaapasharavajraparashvathaanga-shoolaadimadhyasri'nidand'adharaishcha hastaih' . panchaananam dhavaladamsht'ramagaadhanetram tvaamanjanaabhamaribheeshanamaashrayaamah' .. 33.. hastairabheevaraparashvathakri'shnasaara-yuktaishchaturbhirabhishobhitamaananaishcha . tvaam poojayanniha sahasradalaabjasamstham vaanchhaam vrajeddashabhiraavaranairupetam .. 34.. kaalyaadyaabhih' parivri'tatanum shaktibhirdiggataabhi- stanmadhyasthaih' parichitatanum bheeshanaadyaishcha randhraih' . braahmyaadyaabhirdishi dishi tanum(vri'tam) maatri'bhirlokapaalaih' saangam dhyaayan japati sumatirbhootale yah' sa dhanyah' .. 35.. kri'tvaa chakram rajobhistava tadanugunaih' karnikaakesaraad'hyam madhye cha dvaadashaaram kri'taniyamavidhih' shod'ashaaram cha baahye . madhye tvaam poojayitvaa dishi dishi paritah' kesareshvasht'ashaktee- richchhaadidvaadashaareshvatha yajati mahaastraani chatvaari dikshu .. 36.. sheshaareshvasht'arundraanvidiguditatanoon bheeshanaabheeshanaadeen baahye'strairaatmadiksthaih' saha kulishamukhairbhautikaadeeni chaasht'au . tasyaadhivyaadhinaashah' sakalamabhimatam shatrunaashashcha sadyah' shaantih' pusht'ishcha vidyaa dhanamaparimitam kshetrasampattirante .. 37.. yastvaam yuddhodyataangam yajati kri'tamatirbhaaskaraadyairganeshaih' kshetreshaih' konasamsthaih' tridashapatimukhairasht'arudraih' pareetam . aadye tajjnyaanaroopaprabhri'tibhirapare veeraghoshaadirudrai-stadbaahyasthaishchaturthadravinapatimukhaih' panchame kaalamukhyaih' .. 38.. shasht'he chochchhushmamukhyairanishamabhimukhaih' saptame vishnumukhyai- ranyasmin teekshnadamsht'raprabhri'tibhiramareshaadibhishchaaparasmin . aadhaare lokapaalairdishidishi dashame saayudhaih' sevyamaanam bhogaanaasvaadya sarvaan bhuvi tanuvirame mokshamaapnoti so'yam .. 39.. chakram sragvajrashakteerd'amaruparashughant'aahikhad'gaprakhet'aan bibhraanam dand'apaashau dhvajanarashirasee chaapabaanau bhujaishcha . dorbhyaam dvaabhyaam mahaastram niyutaravinibham lootamund'aahibhoosham chaarkaabham kund'alaad'hyam kumatavihataye ghoranaatham bhajaamah' .. 40.. vidyunmaalaanalaabham bhujagaparivri'tam bheeshanam nimnanetram shoolam paasham cha ghant'aamanalamasimahaakhet'akau prajvalantau . savye'bheeshaktichaapaana sharaparashurujaa dakshine ghoravaktram paarshve ghoraastramevam niyamitamanasaa samyaje sarvasiddhyai .. 41.. japtvaayutam (tava manoottama)misht'a(manga)yuktam hutvaa sahasra(mapakri'tya)mapaakaroti . sandhyaasu chaasht'asahitam shatamatra japtvaa dhyaayan kuberasadri'sham shriyameti martyah' .. 42.. aadhaaranaabhihri'daye cha gale cha taalu-bhroomadhyamoordhnyakhilashaktipadeshu devam . tejomayam sarati yah' kramashashcha moksham yo vyutkramena sa narah' punareti bhogam .. 43.. yadvaibhavam tava mahaastramahaanubhaavam stotum na mantrapatayastadasheshameeshaah' . kaa shaktiratra vada taadri'shameedri'shaanaam kashchaikadeshaganako ganakeertimeti .. 44.. etaamaghoraastrapadaanuviddhaam yah' strotramaalaam pat'hati trisandhyam . vijitya(nirjitya)shatroon vigataamayo'sau praapnotyasheshaanapi vaanchhitaarthaan .. 45.. .. iti shreeaghorastavah' sampoornah' ..

gaureegireeshastotram

shreeganeshaaya namah' . chandraardhapravibhaasimastakatat'au tandraaviheenau sadaa bhaktaudhapratipaalane nijatanuchhaayaajitaarkaayutau . shri'ngaadristhavivaahamand'apagatau kaarunyavaaraannidhee kalyaanam tanutaam samastajagataam gaureegireeshau mudaa .. 1.. anyonyaarchchanatatparau madhuravaaksantoshitaanyonyakau chandraardhaanchitashekharau pranamataamisht'aarthadau satvaram . shri'ngaadristhavivaahamand'apagatau shri'ngaarajanmaavanee kalyaanam tanutaam samastajagataam gaureegireeshau mudaa .. 2.. saudaryena parasparam pramuditaavanyonyachittasthitau raakaachandrasamaanavaktrakamalau paadaabjakaalankri'tau . shri'ngaadristhavivaahamand'apagatau gangaatat'aavaasinau kalyaanam tanutaam samastajagataam gaureegireeshau mudaa .. 3.. simhokshaagryagatee mahonnatapadam sampraapayantau nataa- namhoraashinivaaranaikanipunau brahmogravishnvarchitau . shri'ngaadristhavivaahamand'apagatau gaangeyabhooshojjvalau kalyaanam tanutaam samastajagataam gaureegireeshau mudaa .. 4.. kastooreeghanasaaracharchitatanoo pratyooyamaanau surai- rastooktyaa pranatesht'apooranakarau vastoopalabdhipradau . shri'ngaadristhavivaamand'apagataavangaavadhootendubhau kalyaanam tanutaam samastajagataam gaureegireeshau mudaa .. 5.. vaaneenirjitahamsakokilaravau paaneekri'taambhoruhau veneekeshavinirjitaahichapalau kshoneesamaanakshamau .

shri'ngaadristhavivaahamand'apagatau tungesht'ajaalapradau kalyaanam tanutaam samastajagataam gaireegireeshau mudaa .. 6.. kaamaapattivibhootikaaranadashau somaardhabhooshojjvalau saamaamnaayasugeeyamaanacharitau raamaarchitaanghridvayau . shri'ngaadristhavivaamand'apagatau maanikyabhooshaanvitau kalyaanam tanutaam samastajagataam gaureegireeshau mudaa .. 7.. dambhaahankri'tidoshashoonyapurushaih' sambhaavaneeyau sadaa jambhaaraatimukhaamarendravinutau kubhaatmajaadyarchitau . shri'ngaadristhavivaahamand'apagatau vaagdaanadeekshaadharau kalyaanam tanutaam samastajagataam gaureegireeshau mudaa .. 8.. shaapaanugrahashaktidaananipunau taapaapanodakshamau sopaanakramato'dhikaaribhiranupraapyau kshamaasaagarau . shri'ngaadristhavivaahamand'apagatau laavanyapaathonidhee kalyaanam tanutaam samastajagataam gaureegireeshau mudaa .. 9.. shonaambhoruhatulyapaadayugulau baanaarchanaatoshitau veenaadhri'ngmunigeeyamaanavibhavau baalaarunaabhaambarau . shri'ngaadristhavivaamand'apagatau tulyaadhikairvarjitau kalyaanam tanutaam samastajagataam gaureegireeshau mudaa .. 10.. iti gaureegireeshastotram sampoornam ..

Uma-Maheshvara Stotra

namah' shivaabhyaam navayauvanaabhyaam parasparaashlisht'avapurdharaabhyaam . naagendrakanyaavri'shaketanaabhyaam namo namah' shankarapaarvateebhyaam .. 1.. namah' shivaabhyaam sarasotsavaabhyaam namaskri'taabheesht'avarapradaabhyaam . naaraayanenaarchitapaadukaabhyaam namo namah' shankarapaarvateebhyaam .. 2.. namah' shivaabhyaam vri'shavaahanaabhyaam virinchivishnvindrasupoojitaabhyaam . vibhootipaat'eeravilepanaabhyaam namo namah' shankarapaarvateebhyaam .. 3.. namah' shivaabhyaam jagadeeshvaraabhyaam jagatpatibhyaam jayavigrahaabhyaam . jambhaarimukhyairabhivanditaabhyaam namo namah' shankarapaarvateebhyaam .. 4.. namah' shivaabhyaam paramaushadhaabhyaam panchaaksharee panjararanjitaabhyaam . prapanchasri'sht'isthiti samhri'taabhyaam namo namah' shankarapaarvateebhyaam .. 5.. namah' shivaabhyaamatisundaraabhyaam atyantamaasaktahri'dambujaabhyaam . asheshalokaikahitankaraabhyaam namo namah' shankarapaarvateebhyaam .. 6.. namah' shivaabhyaam kalinaashanaabhyaam kankaalakalyaanavapurdharaabhyaam . kailaasashailasthitadevataabhyaam namo namah' shankarapaarvateebhyaam .. 7.. namah' shivaabhyaamashubhaapahaabhyaam asheshalokaikavisheshitaabhyaam . akunt'hitaabhyaam smri'tisambhri'taabhyaam namo namah' shankarapaarvateebhyaam .. 8.. namah' shivaabhyaam rathavaahanaabhyaam raveenduvaishvaanaralochanaabhyaam . raakaashashaankaabhamukhaambujaabhyaam namo namah' shankarapaarvateebhyaam .. 9.. namah' shivaabhyaam jat'ilandharabhyaam jaraamri'tibhyaam cha vivarjitaabhyaam . janaardanaabjodbhavapoojitaabhyaam namo namah' shankarapaarvateebhyaam .. 10.. namah' shivaabhyaam vishamekshanaabhyaam bilvachchhadaamallikadaamabhri'dbhyaam . shobhaavatee shaantavateeshvaraabhyaam namo namah' shankarapaarvateebhyaam .. 11.. namah' shivaabhyaam pashupaalakaabhyaam jagatrayeerakshana baddhahri'dbhyaam . samasta devaasurapoojitaabhyaam namo namah' shankarapaarvateebhyaam .. 12.. stotram trisandhyam shivapaarvateebhyaam bhaktyaa pat'heddvaadashakam naro yah' . sa sarvasaubhaagya phalaani bhunkte shataayuraante shivalokameti .. 13.. iti shreeshankaraachaaryakri'tam umaamaheshvarastotram sampoornam .. shreeshaileshabhramaraambaastutih'

Aghora Murti Sahasranama Stotram

atha aghoramoortisahasranaama likhyate - om shreem hreem kleem sauh' kshmeem ghora ghoraaya jvala jvala prajvala prajvala aghoraastraaya phat' svaahaa . . iti moolam . shreebhairavee uvaacha - bhagavansarvadharmajnya vishvaabhayavaraprada . sarvesha sarvashaastrajnya sarvaateeta sanaatana .. 1.. tvameva paramam tattvam tvameva paramam padam . tvatto'pyanyam na pashyaami saaram saarottamottamam .. 2.. puraa'smaakam varo datto devadaanavasangare . tadadya kri'payaa shambho varam naatha prayachchha me .. 3.. shreebhairava uvaacha - bhairavi preyasi tvam me satyam datto varo mayaa . yadadya manasaabheesht'am tadyaachasva dadaamyaham .. 4.. shreedevee uvaacha - shreeshivah' paramaatmaa cha bhairavo'ghorasanjnyakah' . trigunaatmaa mahaarudrastrailokyoddharanakshamah' .. 5.. tasya naamasahasram me vada sheeghram kri'paanidhe . varametanmahaadeva dehi satyam madeepsitam . asmaadvaram na yaache'ham dehi chedasti me dayaa .. 6.. shreebhairava uvaacha - shri'nushvaikaantabhoodeshe saanau kailaasabhoobhri'tah' . devadaanavasangraame yatte datto varo mayaa . varam tatte prayachchhaami chaanyadvaraya me varam .. 7.. shreedevee uvaacha - atah' param na yaache'ham varamanyanmaheshvara . kri'payaa karunaambhodhe vada sheeghram suraarchita .. 8..

shreebhairava uvaacha - tava bhaktyaa braveemyadya aghorasya mahaatmanah' . naamnaam sahasram paramam trailokyoddharanakshamam .. 9.. naatah' parataraa vidyaa naatah' paratarah' stavah' . naatah' parataram stotram sarvasvam mama paarvati .. 10.. akaaraadi kshakaaraantaa vidyaanidhimanuttamam . beejamantramayam gopyam goptavyam pashusankat'e .. 11.. om asya shreeaghoramoortinaamasahasrasya shreemahaakaalabhairava ri'shih', pankti chhandah', aghoramoortih' paramaatmaa devataa . om beejam, hreem shaktih', kuru kuru keelakam . aghora vidyaasiddhyarthe jape paat'he viniyogah' . atha nyaasah' - hraam angusht'habhyaam namah' . hreem tarjaneebhyaam namah' . hroom' madhyamaabhyaam namah' . hraim anaamikaabhyaam namah' . hraum kanisht'hikaabhyaam namah' . hrah' karatalakarapri'sht'haabhyaam namah' . evam hri'dayaadi shad'anganyaasah' . api cha- om namo bhagavate aghoraaya shoolapaanaye svaahaa hri'dayaaya namah' . rudraayaamri'tamoortaye maam jeevaya jeevaya shirase svaahaa . neelakant'haaya chandrajat'ine shikhaayai vashat' . tripuraantakaaya kavachaaya hum . trilochanaaya ri'gyajuh'saamamoortaye netraabhyaam vaushat' . rudraayaagnitrayaaya jvala jvala maam raksha raksha aghoraastraaya hum phat' svaahaa . astraaya phat' . iti hri'dayaadi shad'anganyaasah' evam karanyaasah' . bhoo rbhuvah' svariti digbandhah' . atha dhyaanam . shreechandramand'alagataambujapeetamadhye devam sudhaasravinamindukalaadharam cha . shuddhaakshasootrakalashaamri'tapadmahastam devam bhajaami hri'daye bhuvanaikanaatham .. api cha - mahaakaayam mahoraskam mahaadamsham mahaabhujam . sudhaasyam shashimaulim cha jvaalaakeshordhvabandhanam .. kinkineemaalayaa yuktam sarpayajnyopaveetinam . raktaambaradharam devam raktamaalaavibhooshitam . paadakinkineesanchchhannam noopurairatishobhitam .. dhyaanamaargasthitam ghoram pankajaasanasamsthitam . bhajaami hri'daye devam devam chaaghorabhairavam .. . iti dhyaanam . atha moolamantrah' . aghorebhyo'tha ghorebhyo ghoraghoratarebhyah' . sarvatah' sarvasarvebhyo namaste rudraroopebhyah' .. . iti moolam . atha aghoraaya namah' . om hreem shreem kleem mahaarudro glaum glaam aghorabhairavah' . kshmeem kaalaagnih' kalaanaathah' kaalah' kaalaantakah' kalih' .. 1.. shmashaanabhairavo bheemo bheetihaa bhagavaanprabhuh' . bhaagyado mund'ahastashcha mund'amaalaadharo mahaan .. 2.. ugrograravo'tyugra ugratejaashcha rogahaa . rogado bhogado bhoktaa satyah' shuddhah' sanaatanah' .. 3.. chitsvaroopo mahaakaayo mahaadeeptirmanonmanah' . maanyo dhanyo yashaskartaa hartaa bharttaa . mahaanidhih' .. 4.. chidaanandashchidaakaarashchidullaasashchideeshvarah' . chintyo'chintyo'chintyaroopah' svaroopo roopavigrahee .. 5.. bhootebhyo bhootido bhootyam bhootaatmaa bhootabhaavanah' . chidaanandah' prakaashaatmaa sanaatmaabodhavigrahah' .. 6.. hri'dbodho bodhavaan buddho buddhido buddhamand'anah' . satyapoornah' satyasandhah' sateenaathah' samaashrayah' .. 7.. traigunyo nirguno gunyo'graneergunavivarjitah' . subhaavah' subhavah' stutyah' stotaa shrotaa vibhaakarah' .. 8.. kaalakaalaandhakatraasakartaa hartaa vibheeshanah' . viroopaakshah' sahasraaksho vishvaaksho vishvatomukhah' .. 9.. charaacharaatmaa vishvaatmaa vishvabodho vinigrahah' . sugraho vigraho veero dheero dheerabhri'taam varah' .. 10.. shoorah' shoolee shoolahartaa shankaro vishvashankarah' . kankaalee kalihaa kaamee haasahaa kaamavallabhah' .. 11.. kaantaaravaasee kaantaasthah' kaantaahri'dayadhaaranah' . kaamyah' kaamyanidhih' kaantaakamaneeyah' kalaadharah' .. 12.. kaleshah' sakaleshashcha vikalah' shakalaantakah' . shaanto bhraanto mahaaroopee sulabho durlabhaashayah' .. 13.. labhyo'nanto dhanaadheenah' sarvagah' saamagaayanah' . sarojanayanah' saadhuh' saadhoonaamabhayapradah' .. 14.. sarvastutyah' sarvagatih' sarvaateeto'pyagocharah' . goptaa goptataro gaanatatparah' satyaparaayanah' .. 15.. asahaayo mahaashaanto mahaamoorto mahoragah' . mahateeravasantusht'o jagateedharadhaaranah' .. 16.. bhikshuh' sarvesht'aphalado bhayaanakamukhah' shivah' . bhargo bhaageeratheenaatho bhagamaalaavibhooshanah' .. 17.. jat'aajoot'ee sphurattejashchand'aamshushchand'avikramah' . dand'ee ganapatirgunyo gananeeyo ganaadhipah' .. 18.. komalaango'pi krooraasyo haasyo maayaapatih' sudheeh' . sukhado duh'khahaa dambho durjayo vijayee jayah' .. 19.. jayo'jayo jvalattejo mandaagnirmadavigrahah' . maanaprado vijayado mahaakaalah' sureshvarah' .. 20.. abhayaanko varaankashcha shashaankakri'tashekharah' . lekhyo lipyo vilaapee cha prataapee pramathaadhipah' .. 21.. prakhyo daksho vimuktashcha ruksho dakshamakhaantakah' . trilochanastrivargeshah' trigunee tritayeepatih' .. 22.. tripureshastrilokeshastrinetrastripuraantakah' . tryambakastrigatih' svaksho vishaalaaksho vat'eshvarah' .. 23.. vat'uh' pat'uh' param punyam punyado dambhavarjitah' . dambhee vilambhee vishebhissamrambhee sangrahee sakhaa .. 24.. vihaaree chaararoopashcha haaree maanikyamand'itah' . vidyeshvaro vivaadee cha vaadabhedyo vibhedavaan .. 25.. bhayaantako balanidhirbalikah' svarnavigrahah' . mahaaseeno vishaakhee cha pri'shat'kee pri'tanaapatih' .. 26.. anantaroopo'nantashreeh' shasht'ibhaago vishaampatih' . praamshuh' sheetaamshurmukut'o niramshah' svaamshavigrahah' .. 27.. nishchetano jagattraataa haro harinasambhri'tah' . naagendro naagatvagvaasaah' shmashaanaalayachaarakah' .. 28.. vichaaree sumatih' shambhuh' sarvah' kharvoruvikramah' . eeshah' sheshah' shashee sooryah' shuddhasaagara eeshvarah' .. 29.. eeshaanah' parameshaanah' paraaparagatih' param . pramodee vinayee vedyo vidyaaraagee vilaasavaan .. 30.. svaatmaa dayaalurdhanado dhanadaarchanatoshitah' . pusht'idastusht'idastaarkshyo jyesht'hah' shresht'ho vishaaradah' .. 31.. chaameekarochchayagatah' sarvagah' sarvamand'anah' . dineshah' sharvareeshashcha sanmadonmaadadaayakah' .. 32.. haayano vatsaro netaa gaayanah' pushpasaayakah' . punyeshvaro vimaanastho vimaanyo vimanaa vidhuh' .. 33.. vidhih' siddhiprado daanto gaataa geervaanavanditah' . shraanto vaanto vivekaaksho dusht'o bhrasht'o nirasht'akah' .. 34.. chinmayo vaangmayo vaayuh' shoonyah' shaantiprado'naghah' . bhaarabhri'dbhootabhri'dgeeto bheemaroopo bhayaanakah' .. 35.. tachchand'adeeptishchand'aaksho dalatkeshah' skhaladratih' . akaaro'tha niraakaara ilesha eeshvarah' parah' .. 36.. ugramoortirutsavesha ooshmaamshurri'nahaa ri'nee . kallihasto mahaashooro lingamoortirlasaddri'shah' .. 37.. leelaajyotirmahaaraudro rudraroopo janaashanah' . enatvagaasano dhoortto dhooliraagaanulepanah' .. 38.. aim veejaamri'tapoornaangah' svarnaangah' punyavardhanah' . omkaarokaararoopashcha tatsarvo anganaapatih' .. 39.. ah'svaroopo mahaashaantah' svaravarna vibhooshanah' .

kaamaantakah' kaamadashcha kaaleeyaatmaa vikalpanah' .. 40.. kalaatmaa karkashaangashcha kaaraabandhavimokshadah' . kaalaroopah' kaamanidhih' kevalo jagataampatih' .. 41.. kutsitah' kanakaadristhah' kaasheevaasah' kalottamah' . kaamee raamaapriyah' kuntah' kavarnaakri'tiraatmabhooh' .. 42.. khaleenah' khalataahantaa khet'esho mukut'aadharah' . kham khad'geshah' khagadharah' khet'ah' khecharavallabhah' .. 43.. khagaantakah' khagaakshashcha khavarnaamri'tamajjanah' . ganesho gunamaargeyo gajaraajeshvaro ganah' .. 44.. agunah' saguno graamyo greevaalankaaramand'itah' . good'ho good'haashayo gupto ganagandharvasevitah' .. 45.. ghoranaado ghanashyaamo ghoornaatmaa ghurgharaakri'tih' . ghanavaaho ghaneshaano ghanavaahanapoojitah' .. 46.. ghanah' sarveshvaro jesho ghavarnatrayamand'anah' . chamatkri'tishchalaatmaa cha chalaachalasvaroopakah' .. 47.. chaaruveshashchaarumoortishchand'ikeshashchamoopatih' . chintyo'chintyagunaateetashchitaaroopah' chitaapriyah' .. 48.. chiteshashchetanaaroopashchitaashaantaapahaarakah' . chhalabhri'chchhalakri'chchhatree chhatrikashchhalakarakah' .. 49.. chhinnagreevah' chhinnasheershah' chhinnakeshah' chhidaarakah' . jetaa jishnurajishnushcha jayaatmaa jayamand'alah' .. 50.. janmahaa janmado janyo vri'janee jri'mbhano jat'ee . jad'ahaa jad'asevyashcha jad'aatmaa jad'avallabhah' .. 51.. jayasvaroopo janako jaladhirjvarasoodanah' . jalandharastho janaadhyaksho niraadhiraadhirasmayah' .. 52.. anaadirjagateenaatho jayashreerjayasaagarah' . jhankaaree jhalineenaathah' saptatih' saptasaagarah' .. 53.. t'ankaarasambhavo t'aanuh' t'avarnaamri'tavallabhah' .

t'ankahasto vit'ankaaro t'eekaaro t'opaparvatah' .. 54.. t'hakaaree cha trayah' t'hah' t'hah' svaroopo t'hakurobalee . d'akaaree d'akri'teed'ambad'imbaanaatho vid'ambanah' .. 55.. d'illeeshvaro hi d'illaabho d'ankaaraakshara mand'anah' . d'havarnee dulliyajnyesho d'hambasoochee nirantakah' .. 56.. navarnee shoninovaaso naraagee raagabhooshanah' . taamraapastapanastaapee tapasvee tapasaam nidhih' .. 57.. tapomayastaporoopastapasaam phaladaayakah' . tameeshvaro mahaataalee tameecharakshayankarah' .. 58.. tapodyotistapoheeno vitaanee tryamyabakeshvarah' . sthalasthah' sthaavarah' sthaanuh' sthirabuddhih' sthirendriyah' .. 59.. sthirankri'tee sthirapreetih' sthitidah' sthitivaamstathaa . dambhee damapriyo daataa daanavo daanavaantakah' .. 60.. daanavaanyanee? dharmaadharmo dharmagatirdhanavaandhanavallabhah' . dhanurdharo dhanurdhanyo dheeresho dheemayo dhri'tih' .. 61.. dhakaaraanto dharaapaalo dharaneesho dharaapriyah' . dharaadharo dhareshaano naarado naarasorasah' .. 62.. saraso viraso naago naagayajnyopaveetavaan . nutilabhyo nuteeshaano nutitusht'o nuteeshvarah' .. 63.. peevaraanga paraakaarah' parameshah' paraatparah' . paaraavaarah' param punyam paraamoortih' param padam .. 64.. parogamyah' parantejah' paramroopah' paropakri't . pri'thveepatih' patih' pootih' pootaatmaa pootanaayakah' .. 65.. paaragah' paaradri'shvaa cha pavanah' pavanaatmajah' . praanado'paanadah' paanthah' samaanavyaanado varam .. 66.. udaanadah' praanagatih' praaninaam praanahaarakah' . pumsaam pat'eeyaanparamah' paramam sthaanakah' pavih' .. 67.. ravih' peetaananah' peet'ham paat'heenaakri'tiraatmavaan . patree peetah' pavitram cha paat'hanam paat'hanapriyah' .. 68.. paarvateeshah' parvateshah' parveshah' parvaghaatanah' . phanee phanida eeshaanah' phullahastah' phanaakri'tih' .. 69.. phanihaarah' phanimoortih' phenaatmaa phanivallabhah' . balee balipriyo baalo baalaalaapee balandharah' .. 70.. baalako balahastashcha balibhugbaalanaashanah' . baliraajo balankaaree baanahasto'rdhavarnabhri't .. 71.. bhadree bhadraprado bhaasvaanbhaamayo bhramayonayah' . bhavyo bhaavapriyo bhaanurbhaanumaanbheemanandakah' .. 72.. bhoorido bhootanaathashcha bhootalam sutalam talam . bhayahaa bhaavanaakartaa bhavahaa bhavaghaatakah' .. 73.. bhavo vibhavado bheeto bhootabhavyo bhavapriyah' . bhavaaneesho bhagesht'ashcha bhagapoojanaposhanah' .. 74.. makuro maanado mukto malino malanaashanah' . maarahartaa mahodhishcha mahasvee mahateepriyah' .. 75.. meenaketurmahaamaaro maheshvaa madanaantakah' . mithunesho mahaamoho mallo mallaantako munih' .. 76.. mareechih' ruchimaanyogee manjulesho'maraadhipah' . mardano mohamardee cha medhaavee medineepatih' .. 77.. maheepatih' sahasraaro mudito maanaveshvarah' . maunee maunapriyo maasah' pakshee maadhava isht'avaan .. 78.. matsaree maapatirmesho meshopahaaratoshitah' . maanikyamand'ito mantree manipooranivaasakah' .. 79.. mandamunmadaroopashcha menakee priyadarshanah' . mahesho megharoopashcha makaraamri'tadarshanah' .. 80.. yajjvaa yajnyapriyo yajnyo yashasvee yajnyabhugyuvaa . yodhapriyo yamapriyo yaameenaatho yamakshayah' .. 81.. yaajnyiko yajnyamaanashcha yajnyamoortiryashodharah' . ravih' sunayano ratnarasiko raamashekharah' .. 82.. laavanyam laalaso looto lajjaalurlalanaapriyah' . lambamoortivilambee cha lolajihvo lulundharah' .. 83.. vasudo vasumaanvaastuvaagbhavo vat'uko vat'uh' . veet'eepriyo vit'ankee cha vit'apee vihagaadhipah' .. 84..

vishvamodee vinayado vishvapreeto vinaayakah' . vinaantako vinaamshako vaimaaniko varapradah' .. 85.. shambhuh' shacheepatih' shaarasamado vakulapriyah' . sheetalah' sheetaroopashcha shaavaree pranato vashee .. 86.. sheetaaluh' shishirah' shaityah' sheetarashmih' sitaamshumaan . sheeladah' sheelavaan shaalee shaaleenah' shashimand'anah' .. 87.. shand'ah' shant'ah' shipivisht'ah' shavarnojjvalaroopavaan . siddhasevyah' sitaanaathah' siddhikah' siddhidaayakah' .. 88.. saadhyo suraalayah' saumyah' siddhibhooh' siddhibhaavanah' . siddhaantavallabhah' smerah' sitavaktrah' sabhaapatih' .. 89.. sarodheeshah' sarinnaathah' sitaabhashchetanaasamah' . satyapah' satyamoortishcha sindhuraajah' sadaashivah' .. 90.. sadeshah' sadanaasoorih' sevyamaanah' sataangatih' . sataambhaavyah' sadaanaathah' sarasvaansamadarshanah' .. 91.. susantusht'ah' sateechetah' satyavaadee sateeratah' . sarvaaraadhyah' sarvapatih' samayee samayah' svayam .. 92.. svayambhooh' svayamaatmeeyah' svayambhaavah' samaatmakah' . suraadhyakshah' surapatih' sarojaasanasevakah' .. 93.. sarojaakshanishevyashcha sarojadalalochanah' . sumatih' kumatih' stutyah' suranaayakanaayakah' .. 94.. sudhaapriyah' sudheshashcha sudhaamoortih' sudhaakarah' . heerako heeravaamshchaiva hetuh' haat'akamand'anah' .. 95.. haat'akesho hat'hadharo haridratnavibhooshanah' . hitakri'ddhetubhootashcha haasyado haasyavaktrakah' .. 96.. haaro haarapriyo haaree havishmallochano harih' . havishmaanhavibhugvaadyo havyam havirbhujaam varah' .. 97.. hamsah' paramahamsashcha hamseenaatho halaayudhah' . haridashvo haristutyo herambo lambitodarah' .. 98.. kshamaapatih' kshamah' kshaantah' kshuraadhaaro'kshibheemakah' . kshitinaathah' kshanesht'ashcha kshanavaayuh' kshavah' kshatah' .. 99.. ksheenashcha kshanikah' kshaamah' kshavarnaamri'tapeet'hakah' . akaaraadi kshakaaraantaa vidyaamaalaavibhooshanah' .. 100.. svara vyanjana bhooshaad'hyo hrasva deergha vibhooshanah' . om kshmri'm mahaabhairaveshee om shreem bhairavapoorvakah' .. 101.. om hreem vat'ukabhaavesho om hreem vat'ukabhairavah' . om kleem shmashaanavaasee cha om hreem shmashaanabhairavah' .. 102.. maim bhadrakaalikaanaathah' kleem om hreem kaalikaapatih' . aim sauh' kleem tripureshaano om hreem jvaalaamukheepatih' .. 103.. aim kleem sah' shaaradaanaatho om hreem maartand'abhairavah' . om hreem sumantusevyashcha om shreem hreem mattabhairavah' .. 104.. om shreem unmattachittashcha om shreem um ugrabhairavah' . om shreem kat'horadeshashcha om shreem hreem kat'horabhairavah' .. 105.. om shreem kaamaandhakadhvamsee om shreem kaamaandhabhairavah' . om shreem asht'asvarashchaiva om shreem asht'akabhairavah' .. 106.. om shreem hreem asht'amoortishcha om shreem chinmoortibhairavah' . om hreem haat'akavarnashcha om hreem haat'akabhairavah' .. 107.. om shreem shashaanka vadanah' om shreem sheetalabhairavah' . om shreem shivaarutashchaiva om shreem shaarookabhairavah' .. 108.. om shreem ahamsvaroopashcha om hreem shreemund'abhairavah' . om shreem manonmanashchaiva om shreem mangalabhairavah' .. 109.. om shreem buddhimayashchaiva om shreem bhaimbuddhabhairavah' . om shreem aim kleem naagamoortih' om shreem hreem naagabhairavah' .. 110.. om shreem kleem koormamoortishcha om shreem kri'karabhairavah' . om hreem shreem devadattashcha om shreem kleem dattabhairavah' .. 111.. om hreem dhananjayashchaiva om shreem dhanikabhairavah' . om shreem hreem rasaroopashcha om shreem rasikabhairavah' .. 112.. om shreem sparsharoopashcha om shreem hreem sparshabhairavah' . om shreem hreem kleem svaroopashcha om shreem hreem roopabhairavah' .. 113.. om shreem sattvamayashchaiva om shreem hreem sattvabhairavah' . om shreem rajogunaatmaa cha om shreem raajasabhairavah' .. 114.. om shreem tamomayashchaiva om shreem taamasabhairavah' . om shreem dharmamayashchaiva om heem vai dharmabhairavah' .. 115.. om shreem hreem madhyachaitanyo om shreem chaitanyabhairavah' . om shreem hreem kshitimoortishcha om hreem kshaatrikabhairavah' .. 116.. om shreem hreem jalamoortishcha om hreem jalendrabhairavah' . om shreem pavanamoortishcha om hreem peet'hakabhairavah' .. 117.. om shreem hutaashamoortishcha om hreem haalaakhabhairavah' . om shreem hreem somamoortishcha om shreem hreem saumyabhairavah' .. 118.. om shreem hreem sooryamoortishcha om shreem saurendrabhairavah' . om joom sah' hamsaroopashcha ham sah' jum om mri'tyanjayah' . om chatvaarimshadadhiko om shreem aghorabhairavah' .. 119.. aghorebhyo'tha ghorebhyo ghoraghoratarebhyah' . sarvatah' sarvasarvebhyo namaste rudraroopebhyah' .. 120.. bhairavesho'bhayavaradaataa devajanapriyah' . om shreem hreem kleem kshmyum devee vai aghoradarshanah' .. 121.. om shreem saundaryavaandevo om aghorakri'paanidhih' . sahasranaama iti naamnaam sahasram tu aghorasya jagatprabhuh' .. 122.. tava bhaktyaa mayaakhyaatam trishu lokeshu durlabham . aprakaashyamadaatavyam goptavyam sharajanmanah' .. 123.. balyam balapradam stutyam stavaneeyam stavottamam . pat'hedvaa paat'hayennityam dhyaayechchetasi nityashah' .. 124.. adrasht'avyamadeekshaaya goptavyam pashusankat'e . naatah' parataram kinchitsarvasvam naasti me hri'di .. 125.. punyadam punyamaatmeeyam sakalam nishkalam param . pat'henmantree nisheethe tu nagnah' shreemuktakuntalah' .. 126.. anantam chitsudhaakaaram devaanaamapi durlabham . shaktyaa yukto japennaamnaam sahasram bhaktipoorvakam .. 127.. tatkshanaatsaadhakah' satyam jeevanmukto bhavishyati . bhaume'rka shanivaare tu shmashaane saadhakah' pat'het .. 128.. sadyastasya svayam devo varadastu bhavishyati . dashaavarttam pat'hedraatrau nadeeteereshu dhairyavaan .. 129.. tasya haste sadaa santi tryambakasyaasht'asiddhayah' . madhyaahe shivaraatrau cha nisheethe vividhe pat'het .. 130.. indraadayah' suraganaa vashameshyanti naanyathaa . gurau braahmamuhoorte tu pat'hedbhaktyaa cha saadhakah' .. 131.. yaavadindrah' sabhaamadhye tadagre mookavat bhavet . shukre nadyaa jale mantree pat'hennaamnaam sahasrakam .. 132.. tadaaprabhri'ti trailokyam mohameshyati naanyathaa . bhaume vanaantare mantree pat'hetsandhyaanidhau tadaa .. 133.. shatruh' kaalasamaano'pi mri'tyumeshyati naanyathaa . trisandhyodayakaale tu pat'hetsaadhakasattamah' .. 134.. rambhaadyapsarasah' sarvaa vashamaayaanti tatkshanaat . bhaume madhyaahnasamaye pat'hechcha koopasannidhau .. 135.. sadyo devi mahaantam kaaripumuchchaat'ayeddhruvam . sadyastrivaaram pat'hennaamnaam sahasramuttamam .. 136.. ihaloke bhavedbhogee pare muktirbhavishyati . arkavaare samaalikhya bhoorjatvachi cha saadhakah' .. 137.. kunkumaalaktakastooree gorochana manah'shilaah' .

sarvaadyairvasubhirmantree vesht'ayettaamrarajjunaa .. 138.. dhaarayenmoordhni sadyastu labhetkaamaanyathepsitaan . putraandaaraamshcha lakshmeem cha yasho dharmam dhanaani cha .. 139.. labhate naatra samshayah' satyametadvacho mama . vinaanena mahaadevi pat'hedyah' kavacham shubham .. 140.. tasya jeevam dhanam putraan daaraanbhakshanti raakshasaah' . vinaanena japet vidyaamaghorasya cha saadhakah' .. 141.. tasya kot'i japam vyartham satyametadvacho mama . bahunaatra kimuktena sahasraakhyam stavottamam .. 142.. yadgri'he vaa japedyastu shraavayedvaa shri'noti yah' . sa svayam neelakant'ho'ham tatkalatram maheshvaree .. 143.. idam rahasyam paramam bhaktyaa tava mayoditam . atyantadurlabham naake tathaatyantam maheetale .. 144.. bhoomau cha durlabham devi gopaneeyam duraatmanah' . aghorasya mahaadevi tattvam paramatattvakam .. 145.. ateeva madhuram hri'dyam paraapararahasyakam . vinaa balim vinaa poojaam na rakshyah' saadhakottamah' .. 146.. pat'haneeyam divaaraatrau siddhayo'sht'au bhavanti hi . idam rahasyam paramam rahasyaatirahasyakam .. 147.. aprakaashyamadaatavyamavaktavyam duraatmane . yathesht'aphaladam sadyah' kalau sheeghraphalapradam .. 148.. gopyam guptataram good'ham guptam putraaya paarvati . gopaneeyam sadaagopyam goptavyam cha svayonivat .. 149.. iti shreerudrayaamale tantre bhairava-bhairavee samvaade aghoramoortisahasranaamastavah' sampoornah' ..

Girisha Stotram

shreeganeshaaya namah' . shirogaangavaasam jat'aajoot'abhaasam manojaadinaasham sadaadigvikaasam . haram chaambikesham shivesham mahesham shivam chandrabhaalam gireesham pranaumi .. 1.. sadaavighnadaaram gale naagahaaram manojaprahaaram tanaubhasmabhaaram . mahaapaapahaaram prabhum kaantidhaaram shivam chandrabhaalam gireesham pranaumi .. 2.. shivam vishvanaatham prabhum bhootanaatham sureshaadinaatham jagannaathanaatham . rateenaathanaashankarandevanaatham shivam chandrabhaalam gireesham pranaumi .. 3.. dhaneshaaditosham sadaashatrukosham mahaamohashosham janaannityaposham . mahaalobharosham shivaanityajosham shivam chandrabhaalam gireesham pranaumi .. 4.. lalaat'e cha baalam shivam dusht'akaalam sadaabhaktapaalam dadhaanankapaalam . mahaakaalakaalasvaroopam karaalam shivam chandrabhaalam gireesham pranaumi .. 5.. parabrahmaroopam vichitrasvaroopam suraanaam subhoopam mahaashaantaroopam . gireendraatmajaa sangri'heetaardharoopam shivam chandrabhaalam gireesham pranaumi .. 6.. sadaagangapaanam sumokshaadidaanam svabhaktaadimaanam prabhum sarvajnyaanam . d'amarum trishoolam karaabhyaam dadhaanam shivam chandrabhaalam gireesham pranaumi .. 7.. ajinaadi goham rateenaathamoham sadaashatrudroham shivam nirvimoham . vibhum sarvakaaleshvaram kaamadroham shivam chandrabhaalam gireesham pranaumi .. 8.. dvijanmaanusevam prabhum devadevam sadaabhootasevam ganeshaadidevam . patangaadidevam hiranyaadidevam shivam chandrabhaalam gireesham pranaumi .. 9.. adevapramaaram shivam sarvasaaram naraanaam vibhaaram ganeshaadipaaram . mahaaroshahaaram hyalankaaradhaaram shivam chandrabhaalam gireesham pranaumi .. 10.. naroyastrikaale pat'hedbhaktiyuktah' shivam praapya sadyastriloke prasiddham . dhanam dhaanyaputram kut'umbaadiyuktam samaasaadyamitram sumuktim vrajetsah' .. 11.. iti shreemishrakunjavihaarinaakri'tam gireeshastotram sampoornam . shubham bhooyaat .

Shri Chandramaulipanchakam

shreechandramaulipanchakam 1
sadaa mudaa madeeyake manah'saroruhaantare vihaarine'ghasanchayam vidaarine chidaatmane . nirastatoyatoyamungnikaayakaayashobhine namah' shivaaya saambashankaraaya chandramaulaye .. 1.. namo namo'sht'amoortaye namo namaanakeertaye namo namo mahaatmane namah' shubhapradaayine . namo dayaardrachetase namo'stu kri'ttivaasase namah' shivaaya saambashankaraaya chandramaulaye .. 2.. pitaamahaadyavedyakasvabhaavakevalaaya te

samastadevavaasavaadipoojitaanghrishobhine . bhavaaya shakraratnasadgalaprabhaaya shooline namah' shivaaya saambashankaraaya chandramaulaye .. 3.. shivo'hamasmi bhaavaye shivam shivena rakshitah' shivasya poornavarchasah' samarchaye padadvayam . shivaatparam na vidyate shive jagat pravartaye namah' shivaaya saambashankaraaya chandramaulaye .. 4.. marandatundilaaravindasundarasmitaanano-nmilanmilindavavri'ndaneelaneelakuntalaam shivaam . kalaakalaapasaarineem shivaam cha veekshya toshineem(ne) namah' shivaaya saambashankaraaya chandramaulaye .. 5.. .. iti shreechandramaulipanchakam sampoornam ..

chandrashekharaasht'akam

chandrashekhara chandrashekhara chandrashekhara paahi maam . chandrashekhara chandrashekhara chandrashekhara raksha maam .. 1.. ratnasaanusharaasanam rajataadrishri'nganiketanam sinjineekri'tapannageshvaramachyutaananasaayakam . kshipradagdhapuratrayam tridivaalayairabhivanditam chandrashekharamaashraye mama kim karishyati vai yamah' .. 2.. panchapaadapapushpagandhapadaambujadvayashobhitam bhaalalochanajaatapaavakadagdhamanmathavigraham . bhasmadigdhakalevaram bhavanaashanam bhavamavyayam chandrashekharamaashraye mama kim karishyati vai yamah' .. 3.. mattavaaranamukhyacharmakri'tottareeyamanoharam pankajaasanapadmalochanapoojitaanghrisaroruham . devasindhutarangaseekarasiktashubhrajat'aadharam chandrashekharamaashraye mama kim karishyati vai yamah' .. 4.. yaksharaajasakham bhagaakshaharam bhujangavibhooshanam shailaraajasutaaparishkri'tachaaruvaamakalevaram . kshved'aneelagalam parashvadhadhaarinam mri'gadhaarinam chandrashekharamaashraye mama kim karishyati vai yamah' .. 5.. kund'aleekri'takund'aleshvarakund'alam vri'shavaahanam naaradaadimuneeshvarastutavaibhavam bhuvaneshvaram . andhakaandhakaamaashritaamarapaadapam shamanaantakam chandrashekharamaashraye mama kim karishyati vai yamah' .. 6.. bheshajam bhavaroginaamakhilaapadaamapahaarinam dakshayajnyavinaashanam trigunaatmakam trivilochanam . bhuktimuktiphalapradam sakalaaghasanghanibarhanam chandrashekharamaashraye mama kim karishyati vai yamah' .. 7.. bhaktavatsalamarchitam nidhimakshayam haridambaram sarvabhootapatim paraatparamaprameyamanuttamam . somavaaridabhoohutaashanasomapaanilakhaakri'tim chandrashekharamaashraye mama kim karishyati vai yamah' .. 8.. vishvasri'sht'ividhaayinam punareva paalanatatparam samharantamapi prapanchamasheshalokanivaasinam . kreed'ayantamaharnisham gananaathayoothasamanvitam chandrashekharamaashraye mama kim karishyati vai yamah' .. 9.. mri'tyubheetamri'kand'asoonukri'tastavam

shivasannidhau yatra kutra cha yah' pat'henna hi tasya mri'tyubhayam bhavet . poornamaayurarogitaamakhilaarthasampadamaadaram chandrashekhara eva tasya dadaati muktimayatnatah' .. 10..
.. iti shreechandrashekharaasht'akam sampoornam ..

Shri Chidambareshvara Stotram

om kri'paasamudram sumukham trinetram jat'aadharam paarvateevaamabhaagam . sadaashivam rudramanantaroopam chidambaresham hri'di bhaavayaami .. 1.. vaachaamateetam phanibhooshanaangam ganeshataatam dhanadasya mitram . kandarpanaasham kamalotpalaaksham chidambaresham hri'di bhaavayaami .. 2.. rameshavandyam rajataadrinaatham shreevaamadevam bhavaduh'khanaasham . rakshaakaram raakshasapeed'itaanaam chidambaresham hri'di bhaavayaami .. 3.. devaadidevam jagadekanaatham deveshavandyam shashikhand'achood'am . gaureesametam kri'tavighnadaksham chidambaresham hri'di bhaavayaami .. 4.. vedaantavedyam suravairivighnam shubhapradam bhaktimadantaraanaam . kaalaantakam shreekarunaakat'aaksham chidambaresham hri'di bhaavayaami .. 5.. hemaadrichaapam trigunaatmabhaavam guhaatmajam vyaaghrapureeshamaadyam . shmashaanavaasam vri'shavaahanastham chidambaresham hri'di bhaavayaami .. 6.. aadyantashoonyam tripuraarimeesham nandeeshamukhyastutavaibhavaad'hyam . samastadevaih' paripoojitaanghrim chidambaresham hri'di bhaavayaami .. 7.. tameva bhaantam hyanubhaatisarvamanekaroopam paramaarthamekam . hyanubhootisarvam pinaakapaanim bhavanaashahetum chidambaresham hri'di bhaavayaami .. 8.. vishveshvaram nityamanantamaadyam trilochanam chandrakalaavatamsam . patim pashoonaam hri'di sannivisht'am chidambaresham hri'di bhaavayaami .. 9.. vishvaadhikam vishnumukhairupaasyam trilochanam panchamukham prasannam . umaapatim paapaharam prashaantam chidambaresham hri'di bhaavayaami .. 10.. karpooragaatram kamaneeyanetram kamsaarimitram kamalenduvaktram . kandarpagaatram kamaleshamitram chidambaresham hri'di bhaavayaami .. 11.. vishaalanetram paripoornagaatram gaureekalatram haridambaresham . kuberamitram jagatah' pavitram chidambaresham hri'di bhaavayaami .. 12.. kalyaanamoortim kanakaadrichaapam kaantaasamaakraantanijardhadeham . kapardinam kaamaripum puraarim chidambaresham hri'di bhaavayaami .. 13.. kalpaantakaalaahitachand'anri'ttam samastavedaantavachonigood'ham . ayugmanetram girijaasahaayam chidambaresham hri'di bhaavayaami .. 14.. digambaram shankhasitaalpahaasam kapaalinam shoolinamaprayem . naagaatmajaavaktrapayojasooryam chidambaresham hri'di bhaavayaami .. 15.. sadaashivam satpurushairanekaih' sadaarchitam saamashirassugeetam . vaiyyaaghracharmaambaramugrameesham chidambaresham hri'di bhaavayaami .. 16.. chidambarasya stvanam pat'hedyah' pradoshakaaleshu pumaan sa dhanyah' . bhogaanasheshaananubhooya bhooyah' saayujyamapyeti chidambarasya .. 17.. iti shreechidambareshvarastotram sampoornam .

shreekaasheevishveshvaraadistotram

shreeganeshaaya namah' .. namah' shreevishvanaathaaya devavandyapadaaya te . kaasheesheshaavataare me devadeva hyupaadisha .. 1.. maayaadheesham mahaatmaanam sarvakaaranakaaranam . vande tam maadhavam devam yah' kaasheem chaadhitisht'hati .. 2.. vande tam dharmagoptaaram sarvaguhyaarthavedinam . ganadevam d'hund'hiraajam tam mahaantam svavighnaham .. 3.. bhaaram vod'hum svabhaktaanaam yo yogam praapta uttamam . tam sad'hund'him dand'apaanim vande gangaatat'asthitam .. 4.. bhairavam damsht'raakaraalam bhaktaabhayakaram bhaje . dusht'adand'ashoolasheershadharam vaamaadhvachaarinam .. 5.. shreekaasheem paapashamaneem damaneem dusht'achetasah' . svanih'shrenim chaavimuktapureem martyahitaam bhaje .. 6.. namaami chaturaaraadhyaam sadaa'nimni sthitim guhaam . shreegange bhairaveem dooreekuru kalyaani yaatanaam .. 7.. bhavaani rakshaannapoorne sadvarnitagune'mbike . devarshivandyaambumanikarnikaam mokshadaam bhaje .. 8.. iti kaasheevishveshvaraadistotram sampoornam .

gaureeshvarastutih'

shreeganeshaaya namah' .. divyam vaari katham yatah' suradhunee maulau katham paavako divyam taddhi vilochanam kathamahirdivyam sa chaange tava . tasmaaddyootavidhau tvayaadya mushito haarah' parityajyataa- mittham shailabhuvaa vihasya lapitah' shambhuh' shivaayaastu vah' .. 1.. shreekant'hasya sakri'ttikaa''rtabharanee moortih' sadaa rohinee jyesht'haa bhaadrapadaa punarvasuyutaa chitraa vishaakhaanvitaa . dishyaadakshatahastamoolaghat'itaashaad'haa maghaalankri'taa shreyo vaishravanaanvitaa bhagavato nakshatrapaaleeva vah' .. 2.. eshaa te hara kaa sugaatri katamaa moorghni sthitaa kim jat'aa hamsah' kim bhajate jat'aam na hi shashee chandro jalam sevate . mugdhe bhootiriyam kuto'tra salilam bhootistarangaayate evam yo vinigoohate tripathagaam paayaatsa vah' shankarah' .. 3.. iti gaureeshvarastutih' samaaptaa .

Shri Gaurishastutih

(shishyaasheervachanaatmakastavaah') baalam chaamamaheemahendrasukri'taksheeraabdhimadhyodbhav am somam somashishoottamaanga satatam maulau nidhaayaadaraat . shreematkri'shnamaheepasanjnyamanisham simhaasanaadhyaasinam vidyaa"yurdhananeetibhih' pratipadam gaureesha samvardhaya .. 1.. jitvaa mri'tyumathaapamri'tyumakhilaan rogaamshcha hri'tvaanisham praanamraakhilalokarakshanavidhaavaabaddhadeeksha prabho . shreematkri'shnamaheepatim sasahajam simhaasanaadhyaasinam maarkand'eyamivaadarena satatam gaureesha samvardhaya .. 2.. shauryaudaaryamukhaangunaananitarapraapyaandadatsarva daa praaleyaachalasetumadhyavilasadbhoopaalavaryed'yataam . deerghaayushyamarogataamapi dadachchhreekri'shnabhoopottamam maatraadyaih' satatam kri'paajalanidhe gaureesha samvardhaya .. 3.. senaadheeshasumantribhri'tyasahitam navyopamanyum prabho kri'tvaa deenajanaavanaikanipunam kaarunyavaaraannidhe . baalam kri'shnamaheepasanjnyamanisham dattvaa cha bhaktim sthiraam haryakshaasanasamsthitam sasahajam gaureesha samvardhaya .. 4.. iti shri'ngeri shreejagadguru shreesachchidaanandashivaabhinavanri'simha-bhaarateesvaamibhih' virachitaa shreegaureeshastutih' samaaptaa .

Shri Kalabhairavapancharatnastutih

khad'gam kapaalam d'amarum trishoolam hastaambuje sandadhatam trinetram . digambaram bhasmavibhooshitaangam namaamyaham bhairavaminduchood'am .. 1.. kavitvadam satvarameva modaannataalaye shambhumano'bhiraamam . namaami yaaneekri'tasaarameyam bhavaabdhipaaram gamayantamaashu .. 2.. jaraadiduh'khaughavibhedadaksham viraagisamsevyapadaaravindam . naraadhipatvapradamaashu nantre suraadhipam bhairavamaanato'smi .. 3.. shamaadisampatpradamaanatebhyo ramaadhavaadyarchitapaadapadmam . samaadhinisht'haistarasaadhigamyam namaamyaham bhairavamaadinaatham .. 4.. giraamagamyam manaso'pi dooram charaacharasya prabhavaadihetum . karaakshipachchhoonyamathaapi ramyam paraavaram bhairavamaanato'smi .. 5.. iti shri'ngeri shreejagadguru shreesachchidaanandashivaabhinavanri'simha-bhaarateesvaamibhih' virachitaa shreekaalabhairavapancharatnastutih' sampoornaa .

Aghoramurti Stotram

aghorastotram om shreeganeshaaya namah' . shreebhairava uvaacha- kailaashashikharaaseenam bhaktaanugrahakaamyayaa . paprachchha pranataa devee bhairavam vigataamayam .. 1.. brahmaadikaaranaateetam svashaktyaa nandinirbharam . namaami parameshaanam svachchhandam veeranaayakam .. 2.. shreedevee uvaacha- praayashchitteshu sarveshu samayollanghaneshu cha . mahaabhayeshu ghoreshu teevropadravabhoomishu .. 3.. chhidrasthaaneshu sarveshu upaayam vada me prabho . yenaayaasena rahito nirdoshashcha bhavennarah' .. 4.. shreebhairava uvaacha - shri'nu devi param guhyam rahasyam paramaadbhutam . sarvapaapaprashamanam sarvaduh'khaabhayapradam .. 5.. praayashchitteshu sarveshu teevreshvapi vishodhanam . sarvachchhidraapaharanam sarvaartivinivaaranam .. 6.. samayollanghane ghore japaadeva vimochanam . bhogamokshapradam chaiva sarvasiddhiphalaavaham .. 7.. shatam jaapyena shuddhyanti mahaapaatakino'pi ye . tadarddham paatakam hanti tatpaadenopapaatakam .. 8.. kaayikam vaachikam chaiva maanasam sparshadoshajam . prasaadaadichchhayaa vaapi sakri'jjapena shuddhyati .. 6.. yaagaarambhe cha yaagaante pat'hitavyam prayatnatah' . nitye naimittake kaamye parasyaapyaatmano'pi vaa .. 10.. nichhidrakaranam proktamabhaavaparipoorakam . dravyaheene mantraheene jnyaanayogavivarjite .. 11.. bhaktishraddhaavirahite shuddhishoonye visheshatah' . manovikshepadoshe cha vilome pashuveekshite .. 12.. vidhiheene pramaade cha japtavyam sarvakarmasu . naatah' parataro mantro naatah' parataraa stutih' .. 13.. naatah' parataraa kaachitsamyak satyam giraa priye . iyam samayavidyaanaam raajaraajeshvaree stutih' .. 14.. paramaapyaayanam devi bhairavasya prakeertitam .

preenanam sarvadevaanaam sarvasaubhaagyavardhanam .. 15.. stavaraajamimam punyam shri'nushvaavahitaa priye . om namah' paramaakaashashaayine paramaatmane .. 16.. shivaaya paramam shaantam giraanandapadaaya te . avaachyaaya prameyaaya pramaatre vishvahetave .. 17.. mahaasaamaanyaroopaaya sattaamaatraikaroopine . ghoshaadidashadhaa shabdabeejabhootaaya shambhave .. 18.. namah' shaantograghoraadi mantrasamrambhagarbhine . revateesraja vishrambha samaashleshavilaasine .. 16.. namah' samarasaasvaadaparaanandopabhogine . bhogapaanaye namastubhyam yogeesha poojitaatmane .. 20.. dvayanirmoolanodyogasamullaasitamoortaye . haraprasaravikshobhavispasht'aaksharamoorttaye .. 21.. namo maayaasvaroopaaya sthaanave paramesht'hine . ghorasamsaarasambhogadaayine sthitikaarine .. 22.. kaalaadi kshitiparyantam paaline vibhave namah' . rohanaaya mahaamohadhvaantavidhvamsahetave .. 23.. hri'dayaambujasankochabhedine shiva maanave . bhogamokshaphalapraaptihetuyogavidhaayine .. 24.. namah' paramanirvaanadaayine chandramaulaye . ghoshyaaya sarvamantraanaam sarvavaangmayamoortaye .. 25.. namah' sharvaaya sarvaaya sarvapaapaapahaarine . ravanaaya ravaantaaya namo'taraavaraavine .. 26.. nityaaya suprabuddhaaya sarvaantaratamaaya te . ghoshaaya paranaadaantacharaaya khacharaaya te .. 27.. namo vaakpataye tubhyam bhagaaya pararoopine . ravanaaya rateeshaarngadehine chitrakarmane .. 28.. namah' shailasutaamaatre vishvakartre mahaatmane . namo maarapratisht'haaya sarvantipadagaaya te .. 26.. namah' samastatattvaaya vyaapine chitsvaroopine . khedvaaraaya bhadraaya namaste rooparoopine .. 30..

paraaparaparispandamandiraaya namo'stu te . bharitaakhilavishvaaya yogagamyaaya yogine .. 31..`namah' sarveshvareshaaya mahaahamsaaya shambhave . charvyaaya charvaneeyaaya charvakaaya charaaya cha .. 32.. raveendusandhisamsthaaya mahaachakresha te namah' . sarvaanusyootaroopaaya sarvaachchhaadakashaktaye .. 33.. sarvabhakshaaya sharvaaya namaste sarvaroopine . ramyaaya vallabhaakraantadehaardhaaya vinodine .. 34.. namah' prasannadushpraapasaubhaagyaphaladaayine . tanmaheshaaya tattvaaya vedine bhavabhedine .. 35.. mahaabhairavanaathaaya bhaktigamyaaya te namah' . shaktigarbhaprabodhaaya sharanyaaya shareerine .. 36.. shaantipusht'yaadisaadhyaaya saadhakaaya namo namah' . ravatkund'alineegarbhaprabodhapraaptashaktaye .. 37.. tatsphot'anapat'upraud'haparamaakshararoopine . samastavyastasangrastarashmijaalodayaatmane .. 38.. namastubhyam mahaasenaroopine vishvagarbhine . revaaravasamudbhootavahnijvaalaavabhaasine .. 36.. ghaneebhootavikalpaandhyavishvabandhavilaapine . bhogineespandanaarood'hapraud'hamaalabdhagarvine .. 40.. namaste sarvabhakshaaya paramaamri'talobhine . nabhakot'isamaaveshabharitaakhilasri'sht'aye .. 41.. namah' shaktishareeraaya kot'idvitayasangine . mahaamohasamaakraantajeevavargavibodhine .. 42.. maheshvaraaya jagataam namah' kaaranabandhave . stenonmoolanadakshaikatritaye vishvamoorttaye .. 43.. namaste'stu mahaadevanaamne parasudhaatmane . rugdraavine mahaaveerya ruruvamshavinaashine .. 44.. rudraaya draavitaasheshabandhanaaya namo namah' . dravatyararasaasvaadacharvanodyuktaye namah' .. 45.. namastridashapoojyaaya sarvakaaranahetave . roopaateeta namastubhyam namaste bahuroopine .. 46.. tryambakaaya tridhaa maatashchaarine cha trichakshushe . peshalopaayalabhyaaya bhaktibhaajaam mahaatmanaam .. 47.. durlabhaaya mahaakraantachetasaam tu namo namah' . bhayapradaaya dusht'aanaam bhavaaya bhayabhedine .. 48.. bhavyaaya tvanmayaanaam tu sarvadaaya namo namah' . anoonaam muktaye ghoraghorasamsaaradaayine .. 46.. ghoraatighoramood'haanaam tiraskartre namo'stu te . ityevam stotraraajendram mahaabhairavabhaashitam .. 50.. yogineenaam param saaram na dadyaadyasya kasyaachit . adeekshite shat'he kroore nissatye shuchivarjite .. 51.. naastike cha khale moorkhe pramatte vilupte'lase . gurushaastrasadaachaaradooshake kalahapriye .. 52.. nirdaye chumbake kshudre samayaghne'tha daambhike . daakshinyarahite paape dharmaheene'tha garvite .. 53.. pashoonaam sannidhau devi nochchaaryam sarvathaa kvachit . asya samsmri'tamaatrasya vighnaa nashyanti sarvashah' .. 54.. guhyakaa yaatudhaanaashcha vetaalaa raakshasaadayah' . d'aamaraashcha pishaachaashcha kroorasattvaashcha pootanaah' .. 55.. byaadhidurbhikshadaurbhaagyamaarimohavishaadayah' . gajavyaaghraadayo dusht'aah' palaayante cha sarvashah' . sarve dusht'aah' pranashyanti ityaajnyaa paarameshvaree .. 56.. .. iti aghorastotram samaaptam .. .. shubhamastu ..

Amareshvara Stotram

kri'shnaaveneetat'aavaasa tri'shnaahri'ttusht'amaanasa . traasahaarimahaaveera traahi maamamareshvara .. 1.. aandhradeshakri'taavaasa chaantarasthamahaarasa . duh'khaanmahaashaktidhara traahi maamamareshvara .. 2.. shreedhaanyavaat'ikaakshetraranjanaanarthabhanjana . jananaantatraasahara traahi maamamareshvara .. 3.. naanotpaataprashamana manah'shaantidachintana . adhisht'hitaamarapura traahi maamamareshvara .. 4.. chaamund'aashaktisahita paraajitanijaahita . hitakaarin mahaadheera traahi maamamareshvara .. 5.. pranaveshaadibhih' panchalingaistvaam sahitam na cha . pashyataam bheerarihara traahi maamamareshvara .. 6.. amaraavatyaadhisht'haanamamaraarinishoodanam . vande tvaamakhilaadhaara traahi maamamareshvara .. 7.. sadaa mamaastu yogaste tvadartham me'pi sadgate . deho'yam tisht'hatu hara traahi maamamareshvara .. 8.. praseeda paarvateejaane na jaane'ham shubhaashubham . smaraami tvaam smarahare traahi maamamareshvara .. 9.. aparaadhaanmaanasikaankaayikaanapi vaachikaan . kshamasva svajanaadhaara traahi maamamareshvara .. 10.. doshaa asheshaa mama ye te nashyantu sadaa'bhaye . tvayyastu hri'dayam taara traahi maamamareshvara .. 11.. iti shreevaasudevaanandasarasvateevirachitam shreemadamareshvarastotram sampoornam .

Directions

One has to recite these prayers with full faith and sincerity and utmost devotion. Shiva is also called Ashutosh, one who can be pleased easily. So recite with pure heart and you will get divine blessings of the Lord. He will protect the worshipper in every calamity.